ADDICTED TO
SCRAPS

12 Vibrant Quilt Projects

Bonnie K. Hunter

KANSAS CITY
STAR QUILTS
an imprint of C&T Publishing

Text copyright © 2016 by Bonnie K. Hunter

Photography and artwork copyright © 2016 by C&T Publishing, Inc.

Publisher: Amy Marson

Creative Director: Gailen Runge

Editor: Liz Aneloski

Technical Editors: Ellen Pahl and Debbie Rodgers

Cover/Book Designer: April Mostek

Production Coordinators: Freesia Pearson Blizard and Tim Manibusan

Production Editors: Jennifer Warren and Nicole Rolandelli

Illustrator: Valyrie Gillum

Photo Assistant: Carly Jean Marin

Quilt photography by Diane Pedersen, unless otherwise noted

Published by Kansas City Star Quilts, an imprint of
C&T Publishing, Inc., P.O. Box 1456, Lafayette, CA 94549

Library of Congress Cataloging-in-Publication Data

Names: Hunter, Bonnie K., author.

Title: Addicted to scraps : 12 vibrant quilt projects / Bonnie K.
Hunter.

Description: Lafayette, CA : C&T Publishing, Inc., [2016] | Includes
bibliographical references.

Identifiers: LCCN 2016009733 | ISBN 9781617453038 (soft cover)

Subjects: LCSH: Quilting--Patterns. | Patchwork quilts.

Classification: LCC TT835 .H8536 2016 | DDC 746.46--dc23

LC record available at https://lccn.loc.gov/2016009733

Printed in the USA

10 9

Dedication

As my life winds its way from year to year, one thing has been constant—my love of fabric and thread, color, texture, design, and the unquenchable urge to create something beautiful out of otherwise ordinary fabric scraps.

I have spent my life being busy. And I don't mean busy in the "normal" sense of the word. Inside this middle-aged woman is the ten-year-old girl who came home with a report card annotated with "Bonnie is bright and cheerful, with much potential *if only* we could contain that extra energy and get her to slow down and focus. ..."

Not much has changed since that fourth-grade report card. I have not slowed down. I have more ideas waiting to be quilts than I have time to make them. And I am happy as the proverbial clam when I am left to create at the beat of my own drummer on overdrive.

My family and friends are no longer driven nuts by my need to constantly cut and sew, design and create, and always go, go, go. They have, over time, come to accept me and have encouraged me to take this excess energy and run with it. They simply nod their heads; they smile—they know me all so well. That's just Bonnie at her "normal."

I dedicate this book to these friends who have not given up on me through the past year of this transition. I promise, those lunches and sew dates we had to put off due to deadlines will be made up for! Thank heavens for emails, phone calls, and Facebook messages that keep us in contact on a regular basis while deadlines are met. I cherish you!

To my readers, who have followed my journey on my blog, quiltville.blogspot.com, over the past eleven years—I wouldn't be here without your encouragement and support. We've done this together! It's been so fun having you along through this incredible journey.

To my family—my husband, Dave, and my sons, Jason and Jeff—I love you beyond measure!

Acknowledgments

Addicted to Scraps is my seventh publication under the Kansas City Star label, and I am honored to now be a part of the C&T Publishing family with Kansas City Star Quilts as an imprint.

My sincere thanks to those who helped me put this book together: April, Carly, Debbie, Diane, Ellen, Freesia, Jennifer, Liz, Nicole, Tim, and Valyrie. Writing for a new publisher can be a scary experience, and I thank you for your patience and incredible welcome as I learn new ways to do things. It's a different dance, and I continue to learn new steps along the way.

Through the publishing of this book, one thing has stuck with me: Don't be afraid of new opportunities. Don't just stay with the comfortable. There is no growth without struggle. Life is not about finding your bliss; go out and CREATE IT!

—*Bonnie K. Hunter*

Contents

PROJECTS

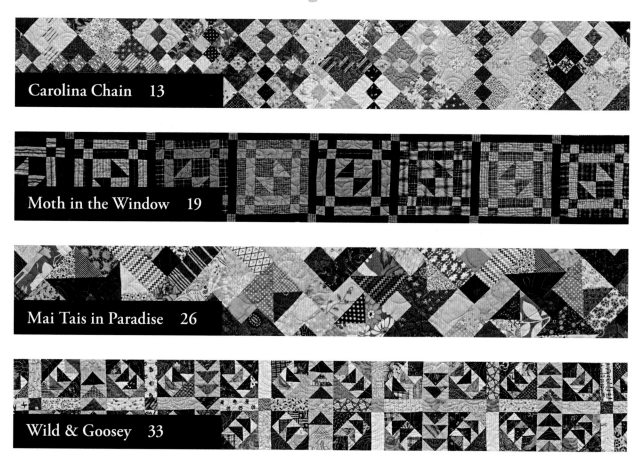

Foreword

I am completely and utterly Addicted to Scraps!

And I know I am not the only one. Do you feel the way I do about scrap quilts?

The first patchwork quilt in my life, as far back as I can remember, was a battered and tattered scrap quilt—a Triple Irish Chain made by some unknown quilter, though it had been passed down through my father's side of the family. Was it a great-aunt? No one seems to remember. Too much time passed without that information being handed down.

I have fond, vivid memories of family vacations at the beach in Santa Cruz, California. My two brothers and I played in the water along the shore of the cold Pacific Ocean until, with teeth chattering and lips blue, we ran back up to the warmth of the sun-soaked sand and flung ourselves on top of this quilt to dry off.

Nose pressed to the tiny squares, I inspected each piece, every print, and every stitch.

Many years later when I was in my twenties, I rescued that quilt from the trunk of my dad's car. By that time I was a budding novice quilter, interested in quilt history and appalled that we had treated this quilt thusly.

But you know what? That quilt has had a lifetime of love and memories. Even in its shredded state, just like the Velveteen Rabbit from the beloved children's story, it knew it was loved due to spots wearing thin, binding coming undone, and fabrics giving way to disintegration after generations of covering family members while they slept and dreamed deeply.

This simple quilt was the start of my exciting journey with scrap quilting.

In 2009, I was contacted by *Quiltmaker Magazine* and asked if I could write a column and design a block for each issue. The column focused on the use of scraps and presented block ideas to help readers find easy ways to use these precious bits. My first "Addicted to Scraps" column appeared in the January/February 2010 issue and continues through today.

I also participate in *Quiltmaker's 100 Blocks* magazines. But these blocks can't simply remain blocks! They have constantly called to me to be made into *real* quilts. *Addicted to Scraps* uses many of the blocks from my column and the *100 Blocks* issues, taking them from simple block status to full quilt completion status with a variety of settings, giving each one a unique and satisfying finish.

I am hopelessly, completely, utterly, and happily ADDICTED TO SCRAPS!

Basic Sewing Guidelines

The patterns for the quilts in this book are based on rotary cutting and machine piecing methods. It is assumed that the reader has a basic knowledge of quilting techniques and processes. The tools needed are those used for basic quiltmaking: it's necessary to have a sewing machine in good working order (to avoid frustration), but no fancy stitches are necessary—just a good straight stitch. I'll share with you a few additional tips I've picked up along the way to make quiltmaking easier and faster.

That ¼″ Seam Allowance

Accurate cutting and piecing are based on a ¼″ seam allowance. It's important to sew a ¼″ seam with your machine. If you can master this, all your blocks will be the intended size and you'll be able to match points perfectly. Even if your machine foot has a ¼″ guide on it, it's easy to overshoot a ¼″ seam just by the nature of that guide already being "outside" of your ¼″ foot. Many of us have a habit of running the fabric too hard up against the guide, giving a seam that is too wide. Do not trust *any* feet with "built-in" guides until you do a seam test!

For more details on sewing an accurate seam allowance and creating a seam guide, see Setting Your Seam Allowance (page 12). Do what you have to so your units come out to the appropriate size before going any further. You and your quilt will be glad you did!

The Scrap User's System

As a longtime scrap quilter, I needed a method that would keep my scraps readily available for ease in making scrap quilts. I much prefer to be sitting and sewing rather than pressing and cutting from odd-sized pieces of fabric. I realized that if I could tackle the leftover scraps from each project as I finished it, the pieces would be cut and ready for me to sew whenever I had time.

Most of the quilts in this book are made from common sizes of units that are then assembled into blocks. Units are usually created by cutting and sewing squares, rectangles, or triangles cut from strips. These strips are cut in widths that we use all the time in traditional patchwork, and they are the basis of my own Scrap User's System of storing strips in usable sizes so they are ready to go. By precutting my scraps into strips and storing them by size and value or color family, I have the ease of pulling the perfect size and color so I can just sit and sew. It's a scrap user's dream!

Scrap Strip Sizes

I cut fabric pieces that are at least 10″ long into strips that are 1½″, 2″, 2½″, and 3½″ wide. I don't cut new yardage or fat quarters this way, just the scraps that are left over from whatever project I've been working on.

I store the strips by color and value in stacked plastic drawers that live under the table of my longarm quilting machine. I have a drawer for each strip width.

Within each size-labeled drawer, I sort strips into color families. For example, in my 2½″ strip bin are color bundles of blue, green, red, purple, orange, brown, and so on. I stack and roll strips into an oblong bundle (think hot dog bun instead of jelly roll) and place each color family in a one-gallon plastic zipper bag to contain them. This prevents wrinkles, tangled strips, and raveling of the raw edges.

Before I began sorting strips by color, I would have to dig through everything to find the color I was searching for and then iron the strips. But not anymore! I have found what works for me.

I cut smaller fabric pieces and strips less than 10″ long into individual squares and bricks by strip width in the following sizes:

1½″ × 1½″ squares and 1½″ × 2½″ bricks

2″ × 2″ squares and 2″ × 3½″ bricks

2½″ × 2½″ squares and 2½″ × 4½″ bricks

3½″ × 3½″ squares

These shapes work great together. Using the stitch-and-flip method, you have everything you need at hand to create flying geese units and star point units with ultimate variety. Just put the squares and bricks by your machine and start building units whenever you have a few minutes!

Where else can you use precut squares in a variety of sizes? How about block corners, block centers, corner-stones for sashing, and even checkerboard borders? The list is endless.

Anything that is too small or oddly shaped to work as a precut strip is delegated to my string or crumb bins.

Neutrals vs. Colors

When working on a scrap quilt—especially one that uses a lot of busy fabrics in every color under the rainbow with a whole lot of variety—I tend to use background fabrics that have less color than the foregrounds. In modern quilt terms, you might find these fabrics termed "low volume." I simply call them "neutrals."

I love a wide variety of neutrals in a neutral-background quilt. Most of the time when I am thinking "lights," I am thinking mostly in terms of neutrals: white to cream to beige to tan, with some pastels thrown in that are very light—pink, yellow, blue, green, and so forth. But they have to be *very* pale if I am going to use them in a light-toned scrappy background.

When considering a fabric for a background, look at the background, or *ground*, of the fabric itself. That will tell you where it wants to play. For instance, a cream fabric with blue flowers and green leaves will qualify as a background neutral because of the cream ground of the fabric. Black music notes on white? It's a neutral because of the white background. Focus on the ground, not on the print.

How dark will I go on neutrals? Keep in mind the color of a brown paper bag. If I am using many shades of neutrals as a background, the color of a brown paper bag is as dark as I will go. If I go darker than that, it becomes a medium and has crossed over to the foreground side! If you keep the image of a brown paper bag in mind, you'll never go wrong when deciding how dark your neutral background should go.

I tend to think of "darks" more as *colors*. They are everything that is *not* light. That means most mediums read as darks against the neutral lights to me. I will kick mediums to the other side to play their part in the main design as foreground.

Specialty Rulers

fast2cut Bonnie K. Hunter's Essential Triangle Tool

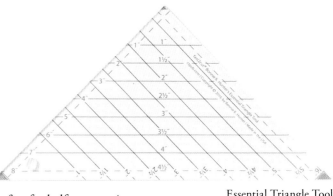

Essential Triangle Tool

With this ruler I have combined the fastest way of making my favorite units accurately—with easy measuring and cutting in multiple sizes—all from one tool. The Essential Triangle Tool is perfect for half-square triangles, quarter-square triangles, and flying geese units, all cut from easy strip widths.

Half-Square Triangles

Use the red lines and numbers.

1. Determine the finished size of your half-square triangle unit and add ½″ for the seam allowance. Cut 1 strip this width of 2 different colors. Example: For a half-square triangle that finishes at 2″, begin with 2½″ strips.

2. Place 2 desired fabric strips with right sides together. Square off one end of the strips.

3. Find the number on the ruler that indicates the finished size of the desired unit. Place that line at the top of the strips as shown, with the solid triangle at the tip of the ruler extending beyond the lower edge of the strips. The vertical edge of the ruler should align with the cut end of the strips. *figure A*

4. Cut through both layers with a rotary cutter.

5. Rotate the ruler, aligning the angled edge of the ruler with the newly cut edge of the strips. The solid triangle at the tip of the ruler will extend beyond the edge of the strips. *figure B*

6. Cut through both layers with a rotary cutter.

7. Return the ruler to Position 1, repeating Steps 3–6 to cut the number of matched triangle pairs needed. Proper cutting and sewing will ensure that the units come out the correct size.

8. Cut and sew a few triangles, chain piecing them one after the other. *figure C*

9. Press and measure. Adjust the seam allowance if needed. Never trust a ¼″ foot. *figure D*

HELPFUL HINTS

• To convert other cutting dimensions for use with this tool, simply find the finished size of the triangle unit needed and add ½″ to this measurement to determine the strip width. If the pattern doesn't state a finished size but gives a cut measurement such as 2⅞″ or 2⅜″, simply subtract ⅜″ from the cut measurement to find the strip width you need.

• If a pattern is having you cut oversized and "sew big to sliver trim down," find the trimmed size. This is the strip width you would cut.

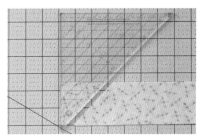

A. Half-square triangles, Position 1

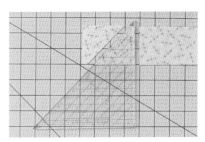

B. Half-square triangles, Position 2

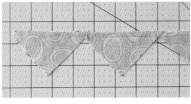

C.

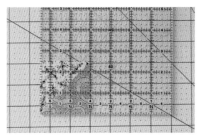

D.

Quarter-Square Triangles

Use the green lines and numbers.

Quarter-square triangles are essential in quilting. They have the straight of grain on the hypotenuse (long side) of the triangle, to prevent stretchy bias edges from being on the outside edge of your quilt or block.

QUARTER-SQUARE TRIANGLES FOR HOUR GLASS UNITS

Layered strips allow you to cut two triangles at once. When you layer two different fabric strips together, you'll cut pairs of triangles already matched together for sewing, making the job extra easy. The numbers along the short side of the ruler will give you the finished unit size, and the numbers in the center tell you what size strip you need to cut.

1. Cut one strip the width you need from each of 2 different colors. The strips shown are for a 4″ finished unit, which uses 2½″ strips.

2. Place the 2 fabric strips with right sides together.

3. Position the ruler so that the desired strip-width line (in this case 2½″) is aligned with the bottom edge of the strips. The solid triangle at the tip of the ruler will extend beyond the strips. *figure A*

4. Cut through both layers on both sides of the ruler with a rotary cutter.

5. Rotate the ruler, aligning the angled edge of the ruler with the newly cut edge of the strips. The solid triangle at the tip of the ruler will extend beyond the bottom edge of the strips. *figure B*

6. Cut through both layers with a rotary cutter along the right side of the ruler.

7. Stitch quarter-square triangle pairs into hour glass halves using a ¼″ seam. Press toward the darker fabric. Proper cutting and sewing will ensure that the units come out the correct size. *figure C*

8. Join the halves to complete each hour glass. Press the seams to one side. *figure D*

FLYING GEESE

Quarter-square triangles and half-square triangles are combined to make flying geese units quickly and easily with no waste, no drawing of lines, and best yet—from strip widths you may already have on hand!

1. Cut quarter-square triangles (center yellow triangle) following Steps 1–5 for hour glass units (at left). Layer like fabric strips together if you need several of the same triangle. Layer different strips to cut 2 different triangles at once. *figure E*

2. Cut half-square triangles (white wing triangles) following Steps 1–7, with one exception. Fold a single fabric strip in half with right sides together rather than stacking 2 separate strips. This will give you 2 mirror-image triangles.

3. Position the right wing triangle and the center triangle with right sides together, matching both the blunt end and the pointy tip. Starting at the blunt tip, stitch the angled side with a ¼″ seam. *figure F*

4. Press the seam toward the wing triangle. *figure G*

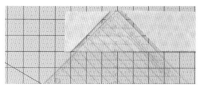

A. Quarter-square triangle cutting, Position 1.

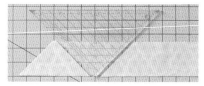

B. Quarter-square triangle cutting, Position 2

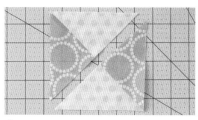

C.

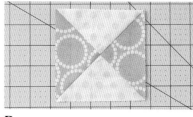

D.

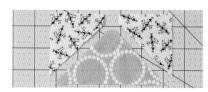

E.

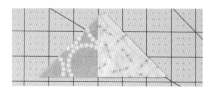

F.

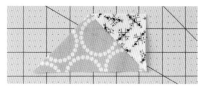

G.

5. Add the left wing triangle to the center triangle with right sides together, matching points and keeping the blunt ends even. Stitch this seam from the bottom point up to the blunt top. Press the seam toward the wing triangle. Trim the dog-ears. *figures H & I*

Use the chart below as a quick reference of strip widths for common sizes of flying geese units.

Finished flying geese unit size	Goose & wing triangle strip width
1″ × 2″	1½″
1½″ × 3″	2″
2″ × 4″	2½″
2½″ × 5″	3″
3″ × 6″	3½″
3½″ × 7″	4″
4″ × 8″	4½″

Bonus Buddy

STITCH-AND-FLIP BONUS HALF-SQUARE TRIANGLE UNITS

Use the Bonus Buddy to quickly mark a second seam line BEFORE you sew stitch-and-flip triangles. Sew just within the drawn lines and you'll get a bonus half-square triangle unit while you're piecing your original project!

The specially measured seam allowance will give you a half-square triangle unit that comes out a perfectly measured and usable size without sliver trimming down. No more wasted triangle scraps!

Bonus triangle units will measure ½″ less than the original stitch-and-flip square you started with and finish at 1″ less than the original square. For instance, if you start with a 2½″ stitch-and-flip square, you will get a 2″ bonus triangle unit that will finish at 1½″ in the quilt.

1. Draw a diagonal line from corner to corner, referring to your stitch-and-flip pattern directions. *figure J*

2. Slide the ruler up and align the Bonus Line with the drawn line. Draw a second line along the long top edge of the Bonus Buddy.

3. The drawn lines are your pressing lines. Stitch between the lines and right next to each drawn line. The lines will end up on *top* of the thread when pressed. *figures K & L*

4. Cut between the lines. *figure M*

> ### Note
> The seam allowance will be $\frac{1}{16}$″ less than a traditional ¼″ seam, but is sufficient to secure the patches. What matters is that your bonus unit comes out the size it should be without having to sliver trim down to the next usable line on the ruler, as you would if you used a full ¼″ seam for each piece. *figure N*

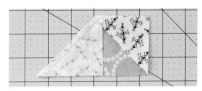

H.

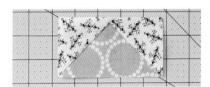

I.

J.

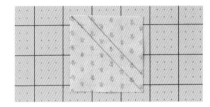

K.

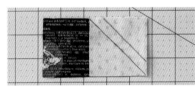

L.

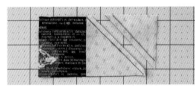

M.

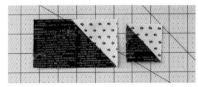

N.

SETTING YOUR SEAM ALLOWANCE

The Bonus Buddy also comes complete with holes to set your seam allowance. You will find holes for ¼″, ⅜″, ½″, and ⅝″ seam allowances.

TIP My favorite seam guide is made from a ¾″ strip of an old hotel room key backed with double stick removable poster tape.

1. To set the proper seam allowance, insert the sewing machine needle into the desired hole width.

2. Lower the presser foot, holding the Bonus Buddy in place. Make sure that the tool is straight on the machine bed.

3. Mark the seam allowance with 3 or 4 layers of masking tape, moleskin, or a stack of post-it notes.

TIP It's best not to cover the feed dogs with any sort of guide. On a digital machine you can needle over so that the tape or guide will not cover the feed dogs or interfere with the foot. On a machine with a drop-front bobbin, consider fitting the guide or tape to fit the top of your bobbin cover only. This way it is easy to change bobbins without having to continually replace your guide.

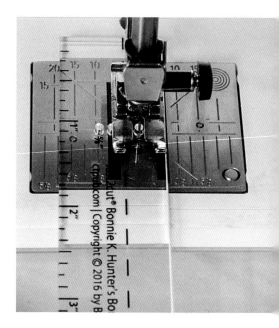

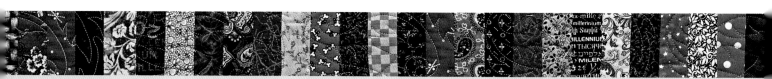

Test That Seam Allowance!

There is more to the perfect unit size than seam allowance alone. Cutting, fabric thickness, and weight of thread are all part of the equation for unit size. The needle hole in the Bonus Buddy is big enough to accommodate different sizes of needles, so there is a little room in the hole to allow you to fine-tune the seam allowance.

To test that your seam guide is in the correct position to give you a perfect ¼″ seam allowance, follow these steps:

1. Stitch a pair of 2½″ × 2½″ squares with right sides together.

2. Press the seam allowances toward the darker square. Measure the piece by placing a rotary ruler on top of the unit. If the unit measures 4½″ across the width of the 2 squares, you are where you should be. If not, adjust your seam allowance by moving the tape (or whatever material you used for your guide).

3. Repeat Steps 1 and 2 until the unit measures 4½″ across.

Carolina Chain

Finished block size: 9″ × 9″ • Finished quilt: 77″ × 89½″

I love the positive/negative aspect of this traditional block, and any quilt that has chains running through it is a definite favorite in my book.

Because I already saved strips in the 2″ width required for this terrifically fun and scrappy quilt, I was sewing in no time! Processing scraps at the end of any project is just part of the routine for me. I don't want a box of random and untamed scrap sizes, so I set to work during the cleanup process to cut anything less than half a fat quarter into strips in a variety of usable sizes.

Having the scraps already cut—ready to go in various widths and with strips on hand in a variety of colors—makes it easy to dive right in to a project. Quilts requiring hundreds of different fabrics would be daunting if I had to take the time to iron fat quarters and cut strips before I could even start to cut the required pieces—not to mention how long it would take before I could actually sew something.

MATERIALS

Yardage is based on 40″-wide fabric.

Dark scraps: 4¼ yards total for blocks

Light neutral scraps: 4¼ yards total for blocks

Blue scraps: 1 yard total for setting triangles

Orange print: ¾ yard for binding

Backing: 7¼ yards

Batting: 85″ × 98″

CUTTING

Dark Chain Quarter-Blocks

From light neutral scraps, cut:

154 matching sets of 2 rectangles 2″ × 3½″ and 2 squares 2″ × 2″

From dark scraps, cut:

154 matching sets of 3 squares 2″ × 2″

Light Chain Quarter-Blocks

From light neutral scraps, cut:

156 matching sets of 3 squares 2″ × 2″

From dark scraps, cut:

156 matching sets of 2 rectangles 2″ × 3½″ and 2 squares 2″ × 2″

Setting Triangles and Binding

From blue scraps, cut:

11 squares 7⅝″ × 7⅝″; cut each square on the diagonal twice to yield 44 side triangles

2 squares 7¼″ × 7¼″; cut each square on the diagonal once to yield 4 corner triangles

From orange print, cut:

9 binding strips 2″ × width of fabric

> **Cutting Note**
> Each block quadrant requires only 2 fabrics in 2 shapes as a set. I worked with 2″ strips, stacking strips 4 layers high to quickly cut the pieces I needed for each block unit. I used as many different fabric pairs as possible to get the look I desired. I placed pieces in zipper plastic bags for easy transport when sewing on the road. Cutting everything ahead meant that I did not need to travel with a rotary cutter or a mat.

Dark Chain Quarter-Blocks

A Sew a dark 2″ × 2″ square to a light 2″ × 3½″ rectangle to make a block row. Press. Make 2 rows.

B Sew a dark 2″ × 2″ square between 2 light 2″ × 2″ squares. Press. Make 1 row.

C Arrange and sew the row of squares between the 2 rows with rectangles, matching the seams to make the quarter-block. Press.

Repeat the steps to make 154 dark chain quarter-blocks. You'll use 144 for the larger blocks; reserve 10 for the pieced setting triangles.

Light Chain Quarter-Blocks

Repeat the steps for the Dark Chain Quarter-Blocks, reversing the value placement so that the quarter-blocks have light chains and dark backgrounds.

D Sew a light 2″ × 2″ square to a dark 2″ × 3½″ rectangle to make a block row. Press. Make 2 rows.

E Sew a light 2″ × 2″ square between 2 dark 2″ × 2″ squares. Press. Make 1 row.

F Arrange and sew the row of squares between the 2 rows with rectangles, matching seams to make the quarter-block. Press.

Repeat the steps to make 156 light chain quarter-blocks. You'll use 144 for the large blocks; reserve 12 for the pieced setting triangles.

Block Assembly

G Arrange and sew 2 light chain and 2 dark chain quarter-blocks together as shown. Press.

Make 72 blocks.

Pieced Setting Triangles

H Sew a blue side setting triangle to adjacent sides of a reserved dark chain quarter-block as shown. Press the seams toward the triangles. Make 10.

I Repeat the process to sew a blue side setting triangle to adjacent sides of a reserved light chain quarter-block as shown. Press toward the triangles. Make 12.

Quilt Assembly

Lay out the blocks in an on-point setting as shown in the quilt assembly diagram; make sure the blocks are oriented correctly, with dark chains running down the quilt from top to bottom and light chains running side by side across the quilt. Fill in around the edges with the pieced setting triangles and corner triangles to complete the dark and light chains.

I like to piece diagonally set quilts into 2 sections and then join the sections. This keeps things from being too unwieldy as the quilt grows.

Starting in a corner, sew the blocks and setting triangles into diagonal rows. Press seams in opposing directions from row to row to facilitate nesting seams. Join the rows into 2 sections; press the seams in one direction. Sew the 2 sections together to complete the quilt center. Press.

Trim It Up!

The outer edges of a diagonally set quilt can be a bit wobbly and may need to be trimmed. Use a 24″ ruler, placing the ruler's ¼″ line where seams cross on the corners of the setting triangles. Straighten the edge with a rotary cutter, leaving a ¼″ seam allowance beyond the block corners around the edges of the quilt. This helps make sure that the quilt corners are also square.

Staystitch the Edges

Diagonally set quilts can also be stretchy. Even though the setting triangles have the straight of grain along the outside edge, the blocks are set on point with the bias grain running from top to bottom and side to side. Stop the stretch by staystitching ³⁄₁₆″ away from the edge of the quilt top, just within the ¼″ seam allowance. Set your sewing machine for a longer stitch length and do not stretch the quilt top when sewing.

Finishing

Layer, quilt, and bind as desired.

I machine quilted *Carolina Chain* with light blue thread in an edge-to-edge design called *Paisley* by Patricia Ritter of Urban Elementz.

I cut binding strips 2″ wide and sew the binding to the quilt with a ¼″ seam. This gives me a ¼″ finished binding that doesn't nip off the points of my blocks.

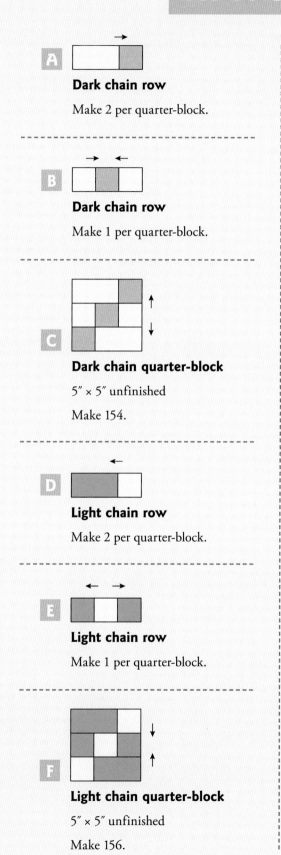

A

Dark chain row

Make 2 per quarter-block.

B

Dark chain row

Make 1 per quarter-block.

C

Dark chain quarter-block

5″ × 5″ unfinished

Make 154.

D

Light chain row

Make 2 per quarter-block.

E

Light chain row

Make 1 per quarter-block.

F

Light chain quarter-block

5″ × 5″ unfinished

Make 156.

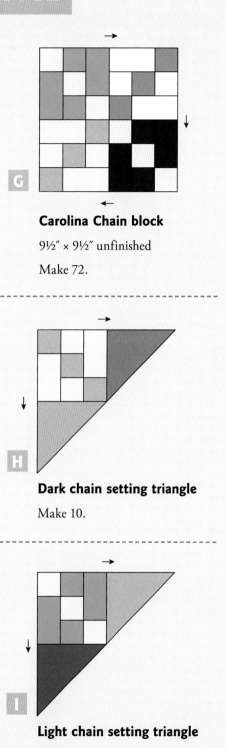

G

Carolina Chain block

9½″ × 9½″ unfinished

Make 72.

H

Dark chain setting triangle

Make 10.

I

Light chain setting triangle

Make 12.

Quilt assembly

Moth in the Window

Finished block size: 8″ × 8″ • Finished quilt: 88½″ × 88½″

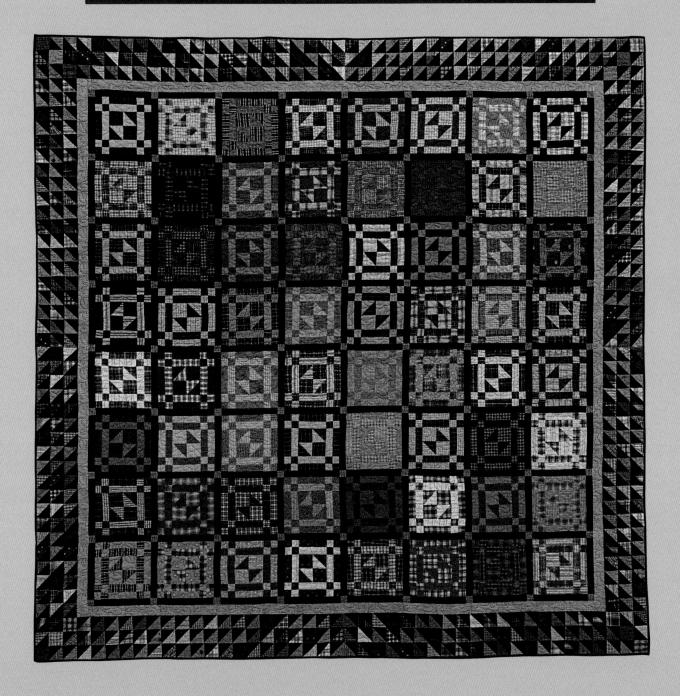

Moth in the Window *is a combination of my best-loved recycled fabrics mixed with solid black and a few other stash yardage favorites.*

My love of working with recycled fabrics from shirts, skirts, blouses, dresses, and even pajama pants knows no bounds. I've been working with recycled fabrics for as long as I have been sewing and quilting, and I love the instantly vintage look it gives my quilts.

Choose fabric carefully when looking for items to recycle. I want the fabric to feel and handle as well as my off-the-bolt fabrics from the quilt shop, so there are a few things I look for. I want good-quality cotton that will work well and play well with my other fabrics. I read labels on clothing just like I would read the label on a can of soup. I want to know what is in there! 100% long-staple Egyptian cotton? Yes, please!

Other blends will work too if they are natural fibers. Cotton/linen is very nice to work with, and a cotton/ramie blend will have a feeling much like homespun. I avoid polyester blends, and I *run* from anything containing even the slightest amount of spandex.

I love tools that work with the sizes of strips I have on hand. Many half-square triangle rulers allow you to work from regular-sized strips with easy math instead of having to deal with that pesky ⅞" measurement. I used my Essential Triangle Tool and 2½" strips for this quilt's many 2" finished half-square triangles.

Traditional rotary cutting measurements are given; modify them as needed for specialty tools. Know your tools and use them to streamline the job when you can.

Feel free to use any of your favorite triangle methods; just be sure to check the dimensions of your sewn units. The triangle units measure 2½" square after sewing and finish at 2" square in the quilt.

MATERIALS

Yardage is based on 40"-wide fabric.

Dark, medium, and light scraps: 8¼ yards total for blocks and outer border

Orange plaid: ¼ yard for cornerstones

Burgundy stripe: 1⅜ yards for sashing

Black solid: 3 yards for sashing, outer border, and binding

White-and-black plaid: ⅝ yard for inner border

Backing: 8 yards

Batting: 97" × 97"

Each block is different, with a combination of 2 fabrics in each block—one for the "moth" and "windows" and one for the background. I paired fabrics based on how they looked, without paying specific attention to lights or darks; instead, I worked more with how colors played off of each other. So let the values and colors fall where they may!

CUTTING

For 1 Block

Cut a total of 64 blocks. If your scraps are less than 32″ wide, simply cut more strips.

From background fabric, cut:

1 strip 1½″ × 32″

2 squares 2½″ × 2½″

1 square 2⅞″ × 2⅞″

From moth and window fabric, cut:

1 strip 1½″ × 32″

1 square 2⅞″ × 2⅞″

Sashing, Borders, and Binding

From burgundy stripe, cut:

6 strips 6½″ × width of fabric

From black solid, cut:

12 strips 1½″ × width of fabric

19 strips 2⅞″ × width of fabric; subcut 240 squares 2⅞″ × 2⅞″

10 binding strips 2″ × width of fabric

From orange plaid, cut:

4 strips 1½″ × width of fabric; subcut 81 squares 1½″ × 1½″

From white-and-black plaid, cut:

8 strips 2″ × width of fabric

From dark, medium, and light scraps, cut:

240 squares 2⅞″ × 2⅞″

12 squares 2½″ × 2½″

> **Note**
> The letters in the following instructions refer to the letters on the piecing diagrams (pages 24 and 25).

Blocks

A Place a moth fabric 2⅞″ × 2⅞″ square and a background 2⅞″ × 2⅞″ square right sides together. Cut on the diagonal from corner to corner to yield 2 matched triangle pairs. Stitch along the diagonal. Press to one side and trim the dog-ears. Make 2. The units will measure 2½″ × 2½″ and finish 2″ × 2″ in the block.

B Lay out these 2 half-square triangle units with the 2 background 2½″ × 2½″ squares as shown. Stitch the units into rows; press the seams toward the unpieced squares. Join the rows to complete the moth unit. Press the seams to one side. The unit will measure 4½″ × 4½″ and finish at 4″ × 4″ in the block.

C Place the window and background 1½″ × 32″ strips right sides together. Stitch together along one long side. Press the seams toward the darker fabric. Cut the strip set into 8 segments 1½″ wide and 4 segments 4½″ wide.

D Sew the 1½″ segments together in pairs as shown to make 4 four-patch units for the block corners. Press the seams to one side.

E Lay out the block units as shown, joining units into rows and joining rows to complete the block. Press the seam allowances toward the longer segments. The block will measure 8½″ × 8½″ and finish 8″ × 8″ in the quilt.

Repeat the steps to make 64 blocks.

Sashing

The sashing is pieced from the burgundy stripe and black solid fabrics with orange plaid cornerstones. The burgundy and black read as one fabric in the photo.

F Sew a black 1½″ strip to each side of a burgundy stripe 6½″ strip. Press the seams toward the center sashing strip. Make 6 strip sets. Cut 144 segments 1½″ wide.

Outer Border

G Place a black 2⅞″ × 2⅞″ square and an assorted 2⅞″ × 2⅞″ square right sides together. Cut on the diagonal from corner to corner to yield 2 matched triangle pairs. Stitch the pairs together along the diagonal. Press the seams toward the black triangle and trim the dog-ears. The units will measure 2½″ × 2½″ and finish 2″ × 2″ in the quilt. Repeat with the remaining squares to make 480 half-square triangle units.

H Join the half-square triangle units into 3 rows of 19 units per row, keeping the black triangles pointing in the same direction. Press the seams in opposite directions from row to row. Join the 3 rows to create a border unit. Make 4. Press.

I Repeat the previous step, reversing the direction of the black triangles. Make 4. Press.

Join a border unit from H to a border unit from I to make 1 complete border. Press the seam open. Make 4.

J Lay out 3 assorted 2½″ × 2½″ scrap squares and 6 of the remaining half-square triangle units as shown. Join the units into rows and press the seams in opposite directions. Join the rows to complete the border corner block. Make 4. Press.

Quilt Assembly

Lay out the blocks in 8 rows of 8 blocks each with the sashing segments and the orange cornerstones. I turned the blocks so that the moth was fluttering at alternating angles across the rows. Join into rows, pressing the seams toward the sashing. Join the rows to complete the quilt center. Press the seams toward the sashing rows.

Inner Border

Join the 8 plaid 2″ inner border strips end to end with diagonal seams to make one long strip. Trim the excess fabric ¼″ beyond the stitching and press the seams open.

Lay the quilt center on the floor, smoothing it gently; do not tug or pull. Measure the quilt through the center from top to bottom. Cut 2 side borders to this length. Sew the side borders to the quilt with right sides together, pinning to match the centers and ends. Ease where necessary to fit. Press the seams toward the borders.

Repeat for the top and bottom borders, measuring across the quilt center and including the borders just added in the measurement. Cut the top and bottom borders to this length and sew to the quilt as before, easing where necessary to fit. Press the seams toward the borders.

Outer Pieced Border

Pin and sew a pieced border to the opposite sides of the quilt center, matching the centers and ends. Ease where necessary to fit. Press the seams toward the inner border.

Add the corner blocks to each end of the top and bottom borders. Press. Pin and sew the borders to the top and bottom of the quilt, matching centers and ends. Ease where necessary to fit. Press the seams toward the inner border.

Finishing

Layer, quilt, and bind as desired.

I machine quilted *Moth in the Window* using tan thread in an edge-to-edge design called *Wandering Leaves* by Susan J. Noyes.

I cut binding strips 2″ wide and sew the binding to the quilt with a ¼″ seam. This gives me a ¼″ finished binding that doesn't nip off the points of the patchwork units in the outer border.

On the Flip Side

Scrappy on the back!

I love the challenge of finding ways for leftover fabrics, blocks, and other units from the top to be showcased on the back. It not only makes the back much more fun to look at but it also keeps me from having to redeposit fabric back into the stash.

I cut shirt backs and fronts in common widths, building columns running from top to bottom down the quilt back. Leftover border triangles were put to good use to separate the columns in places and to add a lot of interest.

Leftover backing margins became the hanging sleeve after quilting.

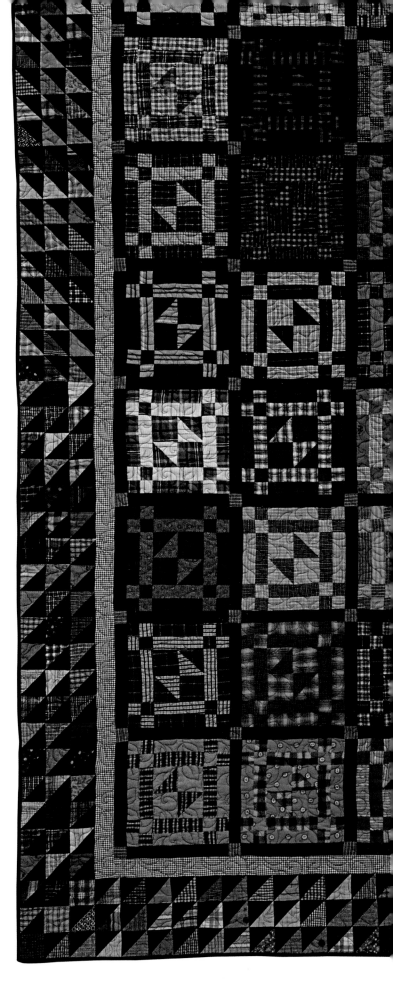

AT A GLANCE

Half-square triangle

2½″ × 2½″ unfinished

Make 2 per block.

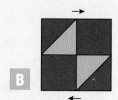

Moth unit

4½″ × 4½″ unfinished

Make 1 per block.

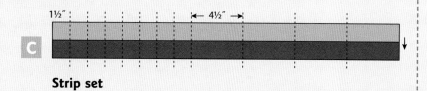

Strip set

Cut 8 segments 1½″ wide and 4 segments 4½″ wide.

Four-patch corner unit

2½″ × 2½″ unfinished

Make 4 per block.

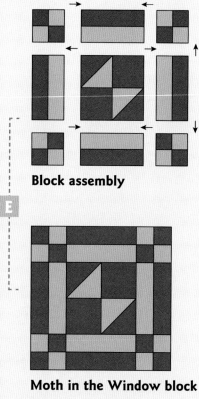

Block assembly

Moth in the Window block

8½″ × 8½″ unfinished

Make 64.

1½″

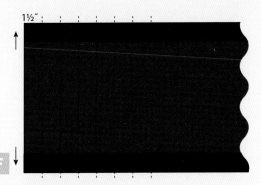

F

Sashing strip set

Cut 144 segments 1½″ wide.

G

Border half-square triangle

2½″ × 2½″ unfinished

Make 480.

H

Border unit 1

Sew 3 rows of 19 units.

Make 4.

I

Border unit 2

Sew 3 rows of 19 units.

Make 4.

J

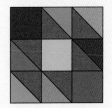

Border corner block

6½″ × 6½″ unfinished

Make 4.

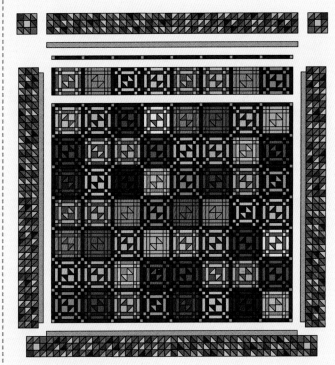

Quilt assembly

Mai Tais in Paradise

Finished block size: 7½" × 7½" • Finished quilt: 55" × 65½"

MATERIALS

Yardage is based on 40"-wide fabric.

Medium to dark scraps: 3 yards total for blocks and binding

Light neutral scraps: 1⅓ yards total for blocks

Black solid: ½ yard for inner border

Aqua dot: 1 yard for outer border

Backing: 4 yards

Batting: 63" × 74"

CUTTING

From medium to dark scraps, cut:

40 squares 3⅞" × 3⅞"; cut diagonally once to yield 80 half-square triangles

20 squares 4¼" × 4¼"; cut diagonally twice to yield 80 quarter-square triangles

104 squares 2" × 2"

80 rectangles 2" × 5"

39 squares 2⅜" × 2⅜"; cut diagonally once to yield 78 half-square triangles

2"-wide strips of random lengths to total about 130" for strip piecing nine-patch units

2"-wide strips of random lengths to total 280" for binding

From light neutral scraps, cut:

80 rectangles 2" × 3½"

28 squares 2" × 2"

20 squares 4¼" × 4¼"; cut diagonally twice to yield 80 quarter-square triangles

1 square 2¾" × 2¾"; cut diagonally twice to yield 4 quarter-square triangles

2"-wide strips of random lengths to total about 100" for strip piecing nine-patch units

From black solid, cut:

6 strips 2" × width of fabric; subcut 1 strip into 8 rectangles 2" × 5"

From aqua dot, cut:

6 strips 5" × width of fabric; subcut 1 strip into 4 squares 5" × 5"

A couple of mismatched charm packs. A pile of random 2" strips in colors and in neutrals. A complicated-looking quilt that really isn't once you get the hang of starting a block with a partial seam. All of my favorite scraps came together in a riotously happy quilt reminiscent of a Caribbean carnival—in a perfect couch size destined for sweet dreaming.

I take best advantage of my scraps when I pair specialty rulers with already-cut strips for quick units on the fly. In this quilt, I used my Essential Triangle Tool with 3½" strips for the large half-square triangles and with 2" strips for the quarter-square triangles.

Traditional rotary cutting measurements are given; modify them as needed for specialty tools. Know your tools and they can save you time.

Note

The letters in the following instructions refer to the letters on the piecing diagrams (pages 31 and 32). In the steps, light neutrals are simply referred to as *light,* and the medium to dark pieces are referred to as *dark.*

Spinning Star Blocks

A Pair up a light quarter-square triangle and a dark quarter-square triangle; sew together so the dark triangle will be on the right side. Press the seam toward the dark triangle. Make 80.

B Place a quarter-square triangle unit and a dark 3⅞" half-square triangle right sides together. Stitch along the diagonal and press the seam toward the larger triangle to make a star point unit. The unit will measure 3½" × 3½" and finish 3" × 3" in the quilt. Make 80.

C Sew a light 2" × 3½" rectangle to the right side of a star point unit. Press toward the rectangle. Make 80.

D Lay out 4 units as shown, placing a dark 2" × 2" square in the center.

E Place the square right sides together with the top star point unit. Sew a partial seam by sewing only halfway across the square; stop sewing and remove the unit from the machine. Finger-press the seam toward the star point unit. The remainder of the seam will be completed later.

F Working counterclockwise, sew the next star point unit to the sewn side of the unit from E. Press toward the star point. Continue to add star point and rectangle units around the center square until all 4 sides have been added; then complete the partial seam. Press.

G Repeat to make 20 blocks. The blocks will measure 8" × 8" and finish 7½" × 7½" in the quilt.

Framed Nine-Patch Blocks

H Sew several strip sets using 2 dark and 1 light 2" strips in each. Press the seams toward the dark strips. Cut 24 segments 2" wide.

HINT Work from *short* strip sets to build the most variety. Make as many strip sets as needed to get the required number of segments.

I Sew several strip sets using 2 light and 1 dark 2" strips in each. Press the seams toward the dark strip. Cut 12 segments 2" wide.

J Join 2 segments from I to each side of a segment from J to make a nine-patch unit. Press. The unit will measure 5" × 5" and finish 4½" × 4½" in the quilt. Make 12.

K Add a dark 2" × 5" rectangle to the top and bottom of the nine-patch unit. Press the seams toward the rectangles just added.

Add a dark 2" × 2" square to each end of 2 dark 2" × 5" rectangles. Press the seams toward the rectangles and sew these units to the sides of the nine-patch unit. Press the seams toward the rectangles. The block will measure 8" × 8" and finish at 7½" × 7½" in the quilt. Make 12.

Pieced Side Triangles

HINT These units will have bias along one edge; handle them carefully.

L Lay out 1 dark and 2 light 2″ × 2″ scrap squares with 3 dark 2⅜″ half-square triangles as shown. Sew the pieces in rows, pressing toward the dark. Join the rows to complete the pieced triangle unit. Make 14.

M Lay out a pieced triangle unit, 2 dark 2″ × 5″ rectangles, 1 dark 2″ × 2″ square, and 2 dark 2⅜″ half-square triangles as shown. Sew the triangles to the ends of the 2 rectangles, pressing toward the triangles. Add the 2″ × 2″ square to the end of the top rectangle, and sew both units to the pieced triangle. Make 14.

Pieced Corner Triangles

N Join a dark 2⅜″ half-square triangle to each end of a 2″ × 5″ rectangle. Press the seams toward the triangles.

Join a light 2⅜″ half-square triangle to opposite sides of a dark 2″ × 2″ square. Press the seams toward the triangles. Add a light 2¾″ quarter-square triangle to the tip. Press the seam toward the triangle just added.

Join the 2 units together. Press the seam toward the rectangle unit. Make 4.

Quilt Assembly

Lay out the Spinning Star blocks and framed Nine-Patch blocks in diagonal rows. Add the pieced side and corner triangles around the edges.

I like to piece diagonally set quilts into 2 sections and then join the sections. This keeps things from being too unwieldy as the quilt grows.

Starting in a corner, sew the blocks and setting triangles into diagonal rows. Press seams in opposing directions from row to row to facilitate nesting seams. Join the rows into 2 sections; press the seams in one direction. Sew the 2 sections together to complete the quilt center. Press.

Trim It Up!

The outer edges of a diagonally set quilt can be a bit wobbly and may need to be trimmed. Use a 24″ ruler, placing the ruler's ¼″ line where seams cross on the corners of the setting triangles. Straighten the edge with a rotary cutter, leaving a ¼″ seam allowance beyond the block corners around the edges of the quilt. This helps make sure that the quilt corners are also square.

Staystitch the Edges

Diagonally set quilts can also be stretchy. Even though the setting triangles have the straight of grain along the outside edge, the blocks are set on point, with the bias grain running from top to bottom and side to side. Stop the stretch by staystitching 3/16″ away from the edge of the quilt top, just within the ¼″ seam allowance. Set your sewing machine for a longer stitch length and do not stretch the quilt top when sewing.

Adding Borders

 Lay out an aqua 5″ × 5″ square, a dark 2″ × 2″ square, and 2 black 2″ × 5″ rectangles as shown. Sew into rows, pressing toward the black rectangles. Join the rows to complete the block. Make 4.

Join the 5 black inner border strips end to end with diagonal seams for a border length approximately 200″ long. Trim the excess fabric ¼″ beyond the stitching and press the seams open.

Join the 5 aqua outer border strips end to end with straight seams for a border length approximately 200″ long. Press seams open.

Stitch the black inner border to the aqua border and press toward the black border.

Lay the quilt center on the floor, smoothing it gently; do not tug or pull. Measure the quilt through the center from top to bottom. Cut 2 side borders to this length.

Measure across the center of the quilt from side to side. Cut the top and bottom borders to this length.

Sew the side borders to the quilt, pinning to match the centers and ends. Ease where necessary to fit. Press toward the borders.

Add a border corner block to each end of both the top and the bottom borders; press toward the block.

Stitch the top and bottom borders to the quilt center, pinning to match centers and ends and easing where necessary to fit. Press toward the borders.

Finishing

Layer, quilt, and bind as desired.

I machine quilted *Mai Tais in Paradise* with a turquoise thread in an edge-to-edge design called *Lavish* by Hermione Agee of Lorien Quilting.

Bind the quilt using a scrappy binding. Join the 2″-wide strips end to end. Press the seams open to make a continuous binding approximately 260″ long. I cut binding strips 2″-wide and sew them to the quilt with a ¼″ seam. This gives me a ¼″ finished binding.

AT A GLANCE

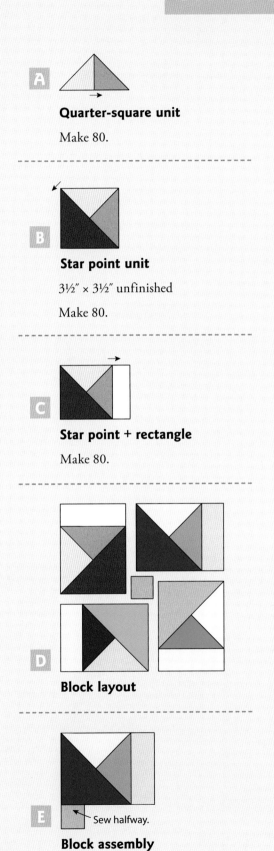

A

Quarter-square unit

Make 80.

B

Star point unit

3½″ × 3½″ unfinished

Make 80.

C

Star point + rectangle

Make 80.

D

Block layout

E

Sew halfway.

Block assembly

Partially sew square.

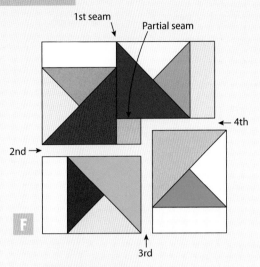

1st seam   Partial seam

2nd →   ← 4th

3rd

F

Block assembly

Add star point units counterclockwise.

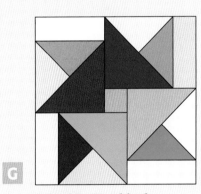

G

Spinning Star block

8″ × 8″ unfinished

Make 20.

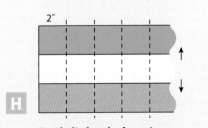

2″

H

Dark-light-dark strip set

Cut 24 segments 2″ wide.

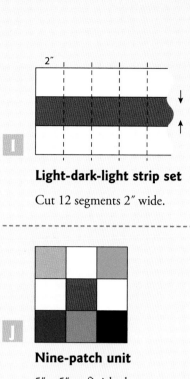

Light-dark-light strip set

Cut 12 segments 2″ wide.

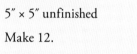

Nine-patch unit

5″ × 5″ unfinished

Make 12.

Block construction

Framed nine-patch unit

8″ × 8″ unfinished

Make 12.

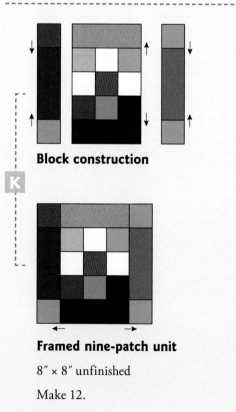

Side triangle construction

Side setting triangle

Make 14.

Corner setting triangle

Make 4.

Corner block

6½″ × 6½″ unfinished

Make 4.

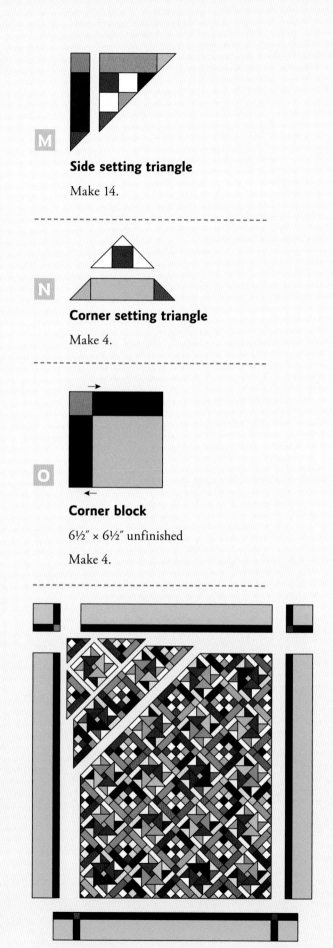

Quilt assembly

Wild & Goosey

Finished block size: 7" × 7" • Finished quilt: 74½" × 83½"

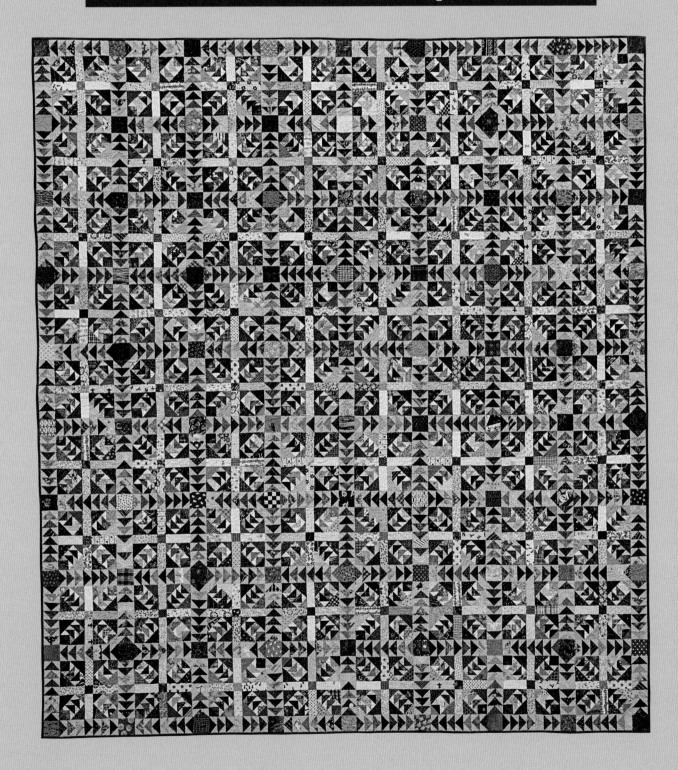

When I am on the road teaching and lecturing, I often travel with a gallon-sized resealable plastic bag of small scraps and a stack of small block foundations for paper piecing. With the help of a borrowed machine on my travels, I am set to go for hours of evening piecing pleasure in the comfort of my hotel room. It helps me happily pass the hours while away from my family. *Wild & Goosey* was pieced over the course of a couple of years during on-the-road sewing.

I love the accuracy of paper piecing. I love that I can get small and scrappy intricate blocks out of a pile of mere nothingness. And the best part of all? As long as those scraps are *bigger* than the space they need to cover, I'm good to go. I don't have to rotary cut anything down to any particular size first, because with paper piecing, we sew first, trim second. It's a no-brainer. Anyone can do it. Give it a try!

All of those triangles trimmed from joining lengths of binding and borders on the diagonal? All of those triangles clipped from behind stitch-and-flip flying geese and snowball units? They were perfectly sized for working into these Wild & Goosey blocks and sashing.

MATERIALS

Yardage is based on 40"-wide fabric. See Note (page 8).

Medium to dark scraps: 7¾ yards total for blocks and sashing

White, cream, and beige scraps: 3¾ yards total for blocks

Yellow solid: 4½ yards for sashing

Purple print: ⅔ yard for binding

Backing: 7 yards

Batting: 82" × 92"

Paper for foundation piecing*

Fabric glue stick

**See Foundations (page 35) for suggestions.*

> **Note**
>
> You will need a huge variety of scraps—there are roughly 2,500 dark triangles and about 1,700 neutral triangles in this quilt! Before purchasing yardage, glean through all the small scraps you've been saving to see what you can sew up into these small quarter-blocks and the sashing. Cut-off triangles, squares, rectangles, pieces, and parts—the more variety, the better. And remember: if it's still ugly, cut it smaller! Just make sure your scraps are a minimum of about 2" × 2".
>
> While the paper-pieced blocks are pieced mainly from small scraps, the yellow in the pieced flying geese sashing came from yardage. I found it easiest to cut the yellow into 2¼" × 2¼" squares, and then cut them on the diagonal to give me slightly oversized triangles to allow for any shifting that can happen with paper piecing. You'll need 1,127 squares 2¼" × 2¼" for a total of 2,254 yellow triangles. But who's counting?!

CUTTING

Cutting does not include the pieces for foundation piecing; use your scraps!

From medium to dark scraps, cut:

90 squares 2½″ × 2½″ for sashing cornerstones

72 squares 1½″ × 1½″ for block centers

From light scraps, cut:

288 rectangles 1½″ × 3½″ for block sashing

From yellow solid, cut:

67 strips 2¼″ × width of fabric; subcut into:

   1,127 squares 2¼″ × 2¼″; cut diagonally once to yield 2,254 triangles

From purple print, cut:

9 binding strips 2″ × width of fabric

Foundations

Copy or trace the required number of foundation patterns onto printer paper, tracing paper, tissue paper, or the foundation paper of your choice.

• Make 288 of the quarter-block pattern (below).

• Make 161 of the sashing pattern (at right).

You might want to try Carol Doak's Foundation Paper (C&T Publishing). I do not recommend vellum or fabric. Vellum curls and shrinks when ironing, and a fabric foundation would make it too bulky with this quilt's small pieces and many seams. I prefer to use paper and remove it before block and quilt assembly.

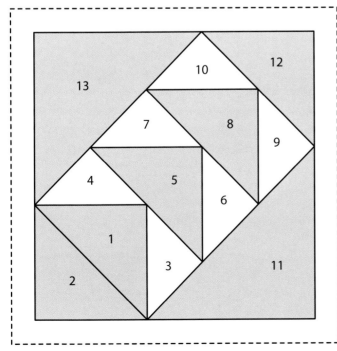

Quarter-block pattern

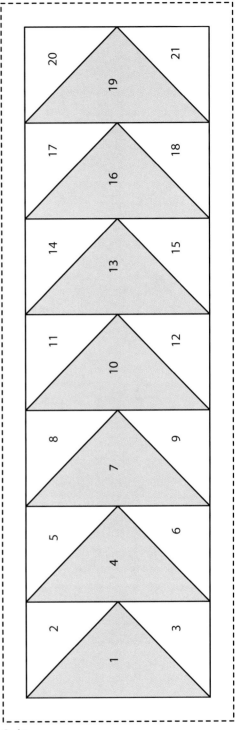

Sashing pattern

Paper Piecing Basics

Many how-to books on paper piecing are available, including best-selling titles from Carol Doak by C&T Publishing. Here are a few helpful hints from my own experience.

Machine Settings

If you have ever had trouble removing the paper from any kind of paper-pieced unit, I can just about guarantee that your stitch length was too long. I recommend setting your machine to a small stitch, starting with 1.5 on a digital machine or about 16 stitches to the inch on a vintage machine. If the paper starts falling off too soon, make your stitch just a bit longer.

I also find it helps to stitch with a larger needle to make bigger holes in the paper. Try a size 14 denim needle.

Sewing on Paper

Begin with the quarter-block foundation. Place the dark fabric for area 1 centered over the space. The wrong side of the fabric should be facing the unprinted side of the foundation. Look through the foundation, holding it up to the light or toward a window, and shift the fabric as needed to make sure there is at least ¼″ of seam allowance extending beyond the line all around area 1. Use a small dot of glue to hold piece 1 in place, or pin. If you pin, do so carefully, as pins can distort the paper.

As you add each fabric piece for the next area, first place it in the correct position on the unprinted side of the foundation, as noted by the numbers on the pattern. It helps to place them where they will be after they have been sewn, keeping cut edges together along the sewing line. Then flip the piece you are adding so that it is right sides together with the piece you are adding it to.

Place a dark fabric piece for area 2 against piece 1 with right sides together, extending it at least ¼″ beyond the sewing line for the seam allowance. Cutting pieces larger

than needed makes positioning easier. Pin the piece in place or hold it in position with your fingers.

Hold the block up toward a window or other light source to help with placement.

Turn the piece over and sew the seam by stitching directly on the line on the printed side of the foundation. Extend the seamline a few stitches into the seam allowance at each end. Future seamlines will cross these and lock them in place. Backstitching is not necessary.

Press the seam after it has been sewn. Use a dry, warm iron, making sure that each seam is pressed completely to the side. Any tucks or pleats you create during pressing will affect the accuracy of the points or corners within your block. *Press!* Do not slide the iron back and forth.

Fold the paper back along the seam just sewn, and trim the seam allowance as each piece is added. Because these blocks are so small, I trimmed a bit less than the traditional ¼″ seam but kept the seam allowances more than ⅛″. I trim with scissors right over my trash can, rather than taking the time to lay everything back on a mat with a ruler and rotary cutter. You will get good at eyeballing where to trim.

Continue in the same manner to add the next light or dark piece in the sequence. Trim and press after sewing each seam.

After adding all the pieces, trim each unit by placing the ¼″ line of a ruler on the block's outermost seamline (solid line), trimming each unit ¼″ beyond the seamline (on the dashed line). At this point, before assembling the quilt, carefully remove all the paper.

If you find yourself with a torn foundation, grab some printer mailing labels (for non-inkjet printers), cut them into narrow strips, and use those as "bandages" to hold your foundations together. These won't melt when touched with the iron, as regular tape will.

Blocks

Refer to Paper Piecing Basics (previous page) as needed.

Piece the quarter-blocks using a variety of dark scraps for the geese that fly corner to corner. I used a wild assortment of light scraps for the wing triangles. The 4 corner triangles surrounding the flying geese are also a fun group of randomly selected dark scraps. Pay attention to fabric value rather than color when piecing.

A Make 288 quarter-blocks. The units measure 3½″ × 3½″ and finish 3″ × 3″ in the quilt.

B Lay out the quarter-blocks with 4 light 1½″ × 3½″ sashing rectangles and 1 dark 1½″ × 1½″ square for the block center as shown. Join the units into rows; press the seams toward the sashing. Join the rows to complete the block. Press. The block will measure 7½″ × 7½″ and finish 7″ × 7″ in the quilt. Make 72.

Flying Geese Sashing

These flying geese soar through a sky of solid yellow in the sashings that frame the Wild & Goosey blocks. Use a lot of variety in choosing the fabrics for each center geese triangle. The wing triangles are all from solid yellow. Most of my geese are dark, but there are a few light ones in there for fun. Just make sure they contrast with the yellow so the geese are visible when flying!

C Make 161 sashing units. The units measure 2½″ × 7½″ and finish at 2″ × 7″ in the quilt.

Quilt Assembly

Follow the quilt assembly diagram to lay out the blocks in 9 rows of 8 blocks each. Add the sashings and corner-stones. Pay close attention to the changing direction of the flying geese in the sashing throughout the quilt.

Join the blocks and sashing into rows; press the seams away from the sashing. Join the rows to complete the quilt top. Press.

Finishing

Layer, quilt, and bind as desired.

I machine quilted *Wild & Goosey* with yellow thread in an edge-to-edge design called *Tea Lights* by Patricia E. Ritter and Valerie Smith of Urban Elementz.

I cut binding strips 2″ wide and sew the binding to the quilt with a ¼″ seam. This gives me a ¼″ finished binding that doesn't nip off the points of the flying geese.

AT A GLANCE

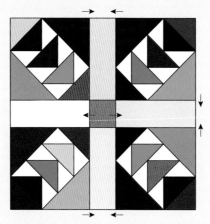

A

Quarter-block

3½″ × 3½″ unfinished

Make 288.

B

Wild & Goosey block

7½″ × 7½″ unfinished

Make 72.

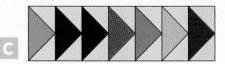

C

Sashing

2½″ × 7½″

Make 161.

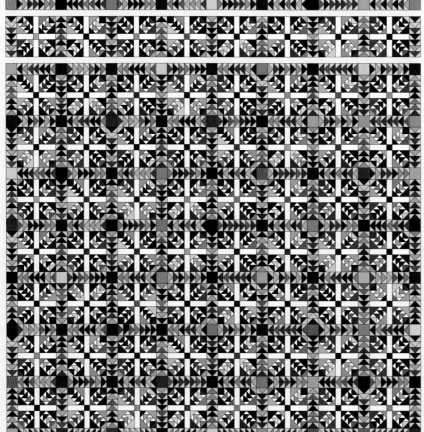

Quilt assembly

Idaho Square Dance

Finished block size: 7″ × 7″ • Finished quilt: 73″ × 73″

Long ago and far away in a land called Twin Falls, Idaho, I came across an antique quilt top made up of little tiny squares of nineteenth-century calicoes and shirting prints. I fell in love. Quilts with small simple squares that chain through the quilt are high on my list of favorites, and the thought of someone piecing these all by hand nearly a century before brought about a feeling of connection that quilters share, both past and present: Love of fabric. Love of color. Love of the simple repetition of needle pulling thread.

And so I bought that top, thinking I could hand quilt it. Well, old fabric can be fragile—often too fragile to quilt. So, instead, I kept the top as inspiration and decided to incorporate the blocks into a diagonal setting with Log Cabin blocks as alternate blocks. I added a piano key border. Can't you see the couples square dancing? I can!

MATERIALS

Yardage is based on 40"-wide fabric.

Blue scraps: 3⅛ yards total for Log Cabin blocks and outer border

Light neutral scraps: 2½ yards total for blocks

Assorted medium to dark scraps: 1¼ yards total for Idaho Square Dance blocks

Red scraps: ⅝ yard total for Idaho Square Dance blocks

Black print: ½ yard for inner border

Red print: ⅝ yard for binding

Backing: 4½ yards

Batting: 81" × 81"

CUTTING

For most efficient cutting, cut scraps into 1½" strips; then subcut the various pieces.

From blue scraps, cut:

36 rectangles 1½" × 7½"

36 rectangles 1½" × 6½"

288 rectangles 1½" × 5½"*

44 rectangles 1½" × 4½"

44 rectangles 1½" × 3½"

44 rectangles 1½" × 2½"

44 squares 1½" × 1½"

From light neutral scraps, cut:

36 rectangles 1½" × 6½"

36 rectangles 1½" × 5½"

36 rectangles 1½" × 4½"

180 rectangles 1½" × 3½"**

36 rectangles 1½" × 2½"

36 squares 1½" × 1½"

1½" strips in random lengths to total approximately 600"

48 squares 1⅞" × 1⅞"; cut diagonally once to yield 96 triangles

From medium to dark scraps, cut:

48 squares 1½" × 1½"

1½" strips in random lengths to total approximately 840"

From red scraps, cut:

25 squares 3½" × 3½"

10 squares 3⅞" × 3⅞"; cut diagonally once to yield 20 setting triangles

1 square 4¼" × 4¼"; cut diagonally twice to yield 4 corner triangles

From black print, cut:

7 strips 2" × width of fabric

From red print, cut:

8 binding strips 2" × width of fabric

*36 are for the Log Cabin blocks, 4 are for the corner blocks, and 248 are for the piano key border.

**36 are for the Log Cabin blocks, and 144 are for the Idaho Square Dance blocks.

Log Cabin Blocks

Note

The Log Cabin blocks are pieced in a counter-clockwise direction. Make sure you piece them all identically. Chain piecing is a big help at this point. If the next rectangle in line does *not* fit your block, double-check your seam allowance to make sure your units are coming out the right size. Measure the unit, not just the seam allowance. Press all seams away from the center square of the block.

A Sew a light 1½″ × 1½″ square to a blue 1½″ × 1½″ center square. Press the seam toward the light square.

Add a light 1½″ × 2½″ rectangle to the unit as shown in the block assembly diagram. Press the seam toward the light rectangle.

Add a blue 1½″ × 2½″ rectangle to the unit, following the pattern counterclockwise. Press.

Add a blue 1½″ × 3½″ rectangle to the unit to complete round 1. Press.

B Continue to add rectangles in this manner until all 3 rounds around the center square are completed. Press. The block measures 7½″ × 7½″ and finishes at 7″ × 7″ in the quilt. Make 36.

Idaho Square Dance Blocks

Four-Patch Unit

Note

Working with short strip sets increases variety, allowing you to use more colors and pairings to add more interest to each block. If your strips are long, cut them into shorter lengths and match them with a variety of other strips for optimum scrapability!

C Sew a dark 1½″ strip to a light 1½″ strip along the long edges to make a strip set. Press the seam toward the light strip. Make several strip sets for maximum variety. Because scrap strips will vary in length, you'll cut different numbers of segments from each strip set. Crosscut each strip set into 1½″-wide segments. Keep sewing and cutting strip sets as needed until you have 240 segments.

VERY IMPORTANT I know it sounds counter-intuitive, but for this block you will press the seams toward the *light* strip in the four-patch strip sets. This is to facilitate seams nesting in the block down the road. Press to the *light*! Or if you prefer, press *everything* open and pin to match seams throughout the construction process.

D Mix and match 2 segments from the strip sets and sew together to make a four-patch unit. Press the seams in one direction to facilitate nested seams later. The units will be 2½″ × 2½″ and finish 2″ × 2″ in the block. Make 120. Set aside 20 of these units for the pieced setting triangles.

Side Unit

E Sew a light 1½″ strip between 2 dark 1½″ strips. Make several strip sets for maximum variety. Press the seams toward the dark strips. Crosscut each strip set into 1½″-wide segments. Keep sewing and cutting strip sets as needed until you have 144 segments.

F Sew a light 1½″ × 3½″ rectangle to the side of a segment from D. Press the seam toward the rectangle. Make 144. Set aside 44 of these units for the pieced setting triangles.

Block Assembly

G Lay out 4 four-patch units, 4 side units, and an assorted red print 3½″ × 3½″ square as shown. Join the units into rows and press. Join the rows to complete the block. The seam on the back of each four-patch may need to be flipped in the other direction to get the seams to nest; this depends on how you place your four-patch to get a pleasing color placement. Press.

H Repeat to make 25 blocks.

Pieced Setting Triangles

Sometimes blocks and units are most easily constructed leaving bias edges on the outside of the block. Such is the case with the setting triangles that frame the center of this quilt. Handle them carefully. The inner border will stabilize the bias edges when it is added.

I Stitch 2 assorted light 1⅞″ triangles to adjacent sides of a dark 1½″ × 1½″ square as shown. Press toward the triangles. Make 48 pieced triangles.

J Lay out a four-patch unit, 2 side units, 2 pieced triangles from I, and a red 3⅞″ triangle as shown. Join the units into rows and press. Join the rows to complete the pieced setting triangle. Make 20.

K Lay out a side unit, 2 pieced triangles, and a red 4¼″ quarter-square triangle as shown. Stitch the pieced triangles to each side of the side unit. Add the red triangle to complete the corner setting triangle. Press. Make 4.

Quilt Assembly

Lay out the Log Cabin blocks and Idaho Square Dance blocks on point in diagonal rows as shown in the quilt assembly diagram. Fill in around the edges of the quilt with the pieced side setting triangles and corner setting triangles.

I like to piece diagonally set quilts into 2 sections and then join the sections. This keeps things from being too unwieldy as the quilt grows.

Starting in a corner, sew the blocks and setting triangles into diagonal rows. Press seams in opposing directions from row to row to facilitate nesting seams. Join the rows together into 2 sections; press the seams in one direction. Sew the 2 sections together to complete the quilt center. Press.

Trim It Up!

The outer edges of a diagonally set quilt can be a bit wobbly and may need to be trimmed. Use a 24″ ruler, placing the ruler's ¼″ line where seams cross on the corners of the setting triangles. Straighten the edge with a rotary cutter, leaving a ¼″ seam allowance beyond the block corners around the edges of the quilt. This helps make sure that the quilt corners are also square.

Staystitch the Edges

Diagonally set quilts can also be stretchy. Stop the stretch by staystitching 3/16″ away from the edge of the quilt top, just within the ¼″ seam allowance. Set your sewing machine for a longer stitch length and do not stretch the quilt top when sewing.

Borders

Inner Border

Join the 7 black print inner border strips end to end with diagonal seams to make 1 long strip. Trim excess fabric ¼″ beyond the stitching, pressing the seams open.

Lay the quilt center on the floor, smoothing it gently; do not tug or pull. Measure the quilt through the center from top to bottom. Cut 2 side borders to this length. Sew the side borders to the quilt with right sides together, pinning to match centers and ends. Ease where necessary to fit. Press the seams toward the borders.

Repeat for the top and bottom borders, measuring across the quilt center and including the borders just added in the measurement. Cut the top and bottom borders to this length and sew to the quilt center as before, easing where necessary to fit. Press the seams toward the borders.

Measure the quilt through the center from top to bottom and take note of this measurement.

Piano Key Border and Corners

L Join 2 blue 1½″ × 1½″ squares together. Press the seam to one side. Add a 1½″ × 2½″ blue rectangle to the right side of the unit. Press the seams toward the rectangle.

Add another blue 1½″ × 2½″ rectangle to the bottom of the unit, pressing toward the rectangle just added.

Continue to add rectangles to 2 sides of the block until the block measures 5½″ × 5½″. Press. The block will measure 5″ × 5″ in the quilt. Make 4.

M Join 2 blue 1½″ × 5½″ rectangles along the long side. Press to one side. Make 124 pairs.

Join the pairs until you have a total of 62 rectangles for a border. Press the seams in one direction. Make 4 borders.

Measure the borders and adjust the length if necessary by taking in or letting out the seams. The length should equal the measurement of your quilt taken after adding the inner border. On-point quilts often have an odd measurement, and piano key borders are very stretchy and forgiving.

Sew the pieced borders to the quilt sides, pinning to match centers and ends. Ease where necessary to fit. Press the seams toward the inner border.

Add the corner blocks to each end of both the top and bottom borders. Press. Sew the borders to the top and bottom of the quilt, pinning to match centers and ends. Ease where necessary to fit. Press the seams toward the inner border.

Finishing

Layer, quilt, and bind as desired.

I machine quilted *Idaho Square Dance* using sand-colored thread in an edge-to-edge design called *Swirling Leaves Revisited* by Jessica Schick.

I cut binding strips 2″ wide and sew them to the quilt with a ¼″ seam. This gives me a ¼″ finished binding.

On the Flip Side

Scrappy on the back!

I love the challenge of finding ways for leftover fabrics, blocks, and other units from the top to be showcased on the back. It not only makes the back much more fun to look at but it also keeps me from having to redeposit fabric back into the stash.

Go for the blues! I tackled a bunch of older blue stash fabrics in an optimum clean-out event, including orphan blocks and leftovers from other projects in the process, just for fun! If there was blue in it or on it, I used it!

AT A GLANCE

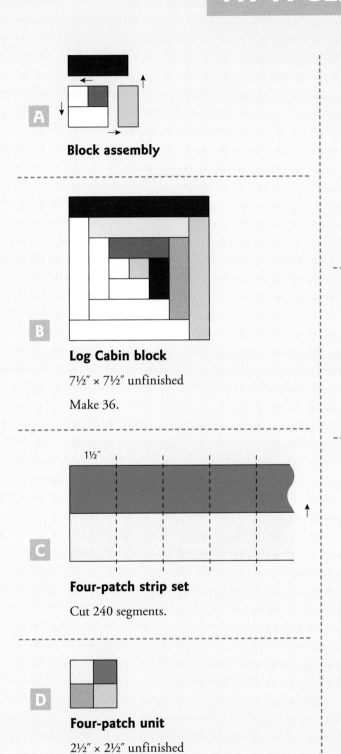

Block assembly

Log Cabin block

7½″ × 7½″ unfinished

Make 36.

Four-patch strip set

Cut 240 segments.

Four-patch unit

2½″ × 2½″ unfinished

Make 120.

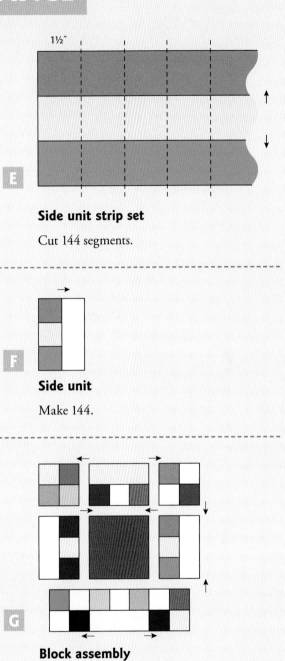

Side unit strip set

Cut 144 segments.

Side unit

Make 144.

Block assembly

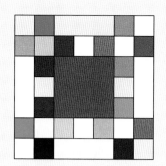

Idaho Square Dance block

7½″ × 7½″ unfinished

Make 25.

Pieced triangle

Make 48.

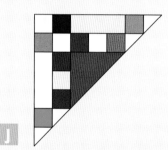

Pieced setting triangle

Make 20.

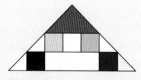

Pieced corner triangle

Make 4.

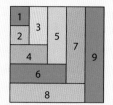

Border corner block

5½″ × 5½″ unfinished

Make 4.

Border unit

Sew rectangles in pairs.

Make 124.

Quilt assembly

Pinwheel Fancy

Finished block size: 6″ × 6″ • Finished quilt: 77″ × 77″

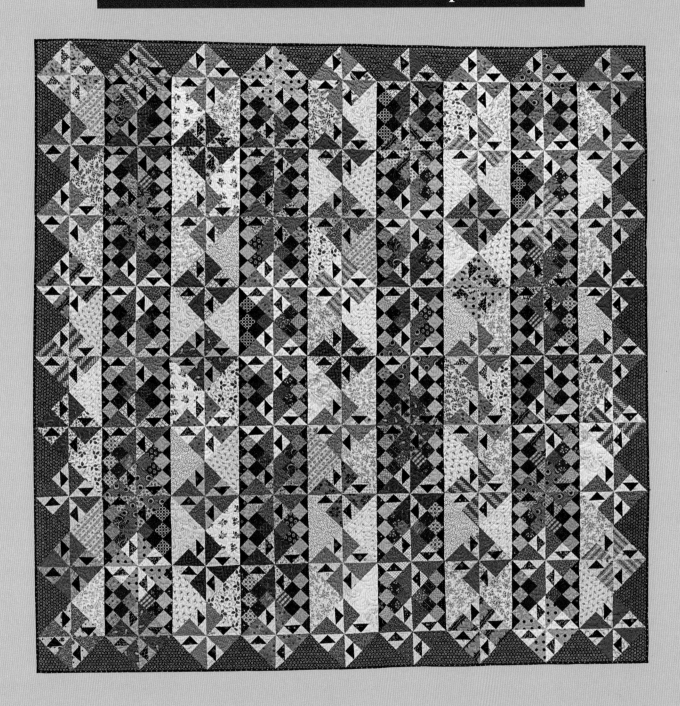

Things that twirl, things that spin! Quilt blocks with motion provide endless possibility for quilt designs from simple shapes and units. Throw in a secondary block, turn the whole thing on point, and you create vertical columns where pinwheels can happily spin away.

I didn't have to do a lot of precutting from fat quarters or yardage to get started. I could easily make batches of pinwheel blocks and setting blocks when I pulled precut strips from my drawers. To read more, see Scrap User's System (page 7).

Using my specialty ruler, the Essential Triangle Tool, for cutting half-square triangles meant that I could use strips in 2″ and 3½″ widths, as is—right out of my Scrap User's System—without having to deal with ⅞″ or ⅜″ measurements.

Traditional rotary cutting measurements are given; modify them as needed for specialty tools. Know your specialty rulers and what they can do for you!

MATERIALS

Yardage is based on 40″-wide fabric.

Blue scraps: 2⅛ yards total for blocks

Black scraps: 1½ yards total for blocks

Light neutral scraps: 3¾ yards total for blocks

Rust scraps: ⅓ yard total for blocks

Red scraps: ½ yard total for blocks

Gold scraps: ⅔ yard total for blocks

Brown print: 1 yard for setting triangles

Black print: ⅝ yard for binding

Backing: 7 yards

Batting: 85″ × 85″

> *Note*
> I used as many fabric scraps as I could within each color family.

CUTTING

Pinwheel Fancy Blocks

From blue scraps, cut:

81 sets of 2 matching 3⅞″ × 3⅞″ squares; cut diagonally once to yield 4 triangles

From black scraps, cut:

81 sets of 2 matching 2⅜″ × 2⅜″ squares; cut diagonally once to yield 4 triangles

From light neutral scraps, cut:

81 sets of 6 matching squares 2⅜″ × 2⅜″; cut diagonally once to yield 12 triangles

Setting Blocks

From black scraps, cut:

64 sets of 2 matching 2⅜″ × 2⅜″ squares; cut diagonally once to yield 4 triangles

From rust scraps, cut:

64 squares 2″ × 2″

From red scraps, cut:

64 sets of 2 matching 2″ × 2″ squares

From gold scraps, cut:

64 sets of 3 matching 2″ × 2″ squares

From light neutral scraps, cut:

32 squares 6⅞″ × 6⅞″; cut diagonally once to yield 64 triangles

Setting Triangles and Binding

From brown print, cut:

8 squares 9¾″ × 9¾″; cut diagonally twice to yield 32 setting triangles

2 squares 5⅛″ × 5⅛″; cut diagonally once to yield 4 corner triangles

From black print, cut:

9 binding strips 2″ × width of fabric

Pinwheel Fancy Blocks

A Pair 4 matching black half-square triangles with a set of matching light triangles. Sew the triangles together to make 4 half-square triangle units. Press the seams toward the black triangle. The units will measure 2″ × 2″ and finish 1½″ × 1½″ in the block.

B Add a matching light triangle to the adjacent sides of the half-square triangle units as shown. Press the seams toward the triangles just added.

C Sew the pieced triangle units to a set of 4 matching blue 3⅞″ half-square triangles to make quarter-blocks. Press the seams toward the blue triangles. The units will measure 3½″ × 3½″ and finish 3″ × 3″ in the block.

D Lay out the 4 quarter-blocks as shown and sew into rows. Press toward the blue triangles. Join the rows to complete the block. Press the seams toward the blue triangles by gently opening the stitches in the center seam allowance to help minimize bulk. The blocks will measure 6½″ × 6½″ and finish 6″ × 6″ in the quilt. Repeat the steps to make 81. Be sure to keep the pinwheels spinning in the same direction for each block.

Setting Blocks

If all the setting blocks were made of identical fabrics, it would be easy to strip piece them, but I wanted them all to be different! I found it easiest to lay out the units in rows and simply join them together the way I wanted them.

E Lay out the 2″ × 2″ squares—1 rust square, 2 matching red squares, 3 matching gold squares—and 4 matching black print triangles as shown. Join into rows and press the seams in opposite directions from row to row. Join the rows and press carefully.

F Sew the pieced triangle to a light 6⅞″ half-square triangle. Press the seams toward the light triangle. The block will measure 6½″ × 6½″ and finish 6″ × 6″ in the quilt. Repeat the steps to make 64 blocks.

Quilt Assembly

Lay out the blocks in diagonal rows, alternating the Pinwheel Fancy blocks and the setting blocks. Fill in around the edges of the quilt with the brown print side and corner setting triangles.

I like to piece diagonally set quilts into 2 sections and then join the sections. This keeps things from being too unwieldy as the quilt grows.

Starting in a corner, sew the blocks and setting triangles into diagonal rows. Press seams in opposing directions from row to row to facilitate nesting seams. Join the rows into 2 sections; press the seams in one direction. Sew the 2 sections together to complete the quilt center. Press.

Trim It Up!

The outer edges of a diagonally set quilt can be a bit wobbly and may need to be trimmed. Use a 24″ ruler, placing the ruler's ¼″ line where seams cross on the corners of the setting triangles. Straighten the edge with a rotary cutter, leaving a ¼″ seam allowance beyond the block corners around the edges of the quilt. This helps make sure that the quilt corners are also square.

Staystitch the Edges

Diagonally set quilts can also be stretchy. Even though the setting triangles have the straight of grain along the outside edge, the blocks are set on point, with the bias grain running from top to bottom and side to side. Stop the stretch by staystitching ³⁄₁₆″ away from the edge of the quilt top, just within the ¼″ seam allowance. Set your sewing machine for a longer stitch length and do not stretch the quilt top when sewing.

Finishing

Layer, quilt, and bind as desired.

I machine quilted *Pinwheel Fancy* with a gold-colored thread in an edge-to-edge design called *Wisteria* by Patricia E. Ritter of Urban Elementz.

I cut binding strips 2″ wide and sew them to the quilt with a ¼″ seam. This gives a ¼″ finished binding that doesn't nip off the points of my blocks.

AT A GLANCE

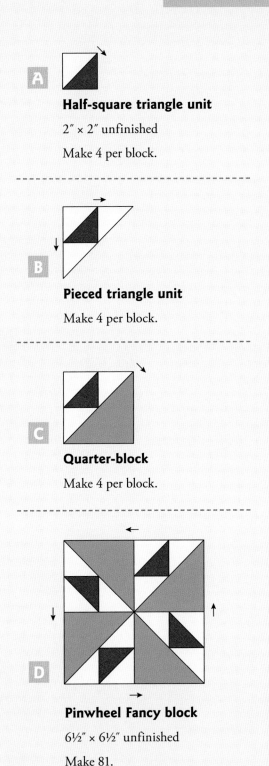

A

Half-square triangle unit

2″ × 2″ unfinished

Make 4 per block.

B

Pieced triangle unit

Make 4 per block.

C

Quarter-block

Make 4 per block.

D

Pinwheel Fancy block

6½″ × 6½″ unfinished

Make 81.

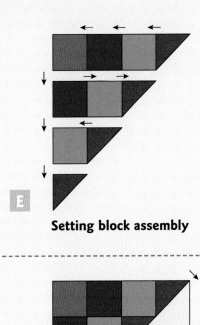

E

Setting block assembly

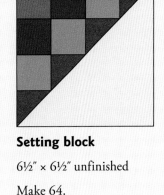

F

Setting block

6½″ × 6½″ unfinished

Make 64.

Quilt assembly

Twirl Around

Finished block size: 6" × 6" • Finished quilt: 83½" × 83½"

Spinning pinwheels dance between simply pieced alternate blocks, leaving stars in their wake as they crisscross across the quilt surface.

Many of the half-square triangles in this sweet quilt were collected as bonus units by saving the trimmed triangle pairs from stitch-and-flip units. I also dug through my 2″ strip stash, pulling a fun selection of light neutrals, pinks, and greens for this project. A batch of pink 3½″ strips became the center squares in the alternate blocks, with shades that range from very light pink all the way to dark berry.

I used my Essential Triangle Tool to cut half-square triangles from 2″ strips without having to deal with odd measurements like ⅜″. This allowed me to cut *more* units easily in no time flat.

Traditional rotary cutting measurements are given; modify them as needed for specialty tools. Know your specialty rulers and how they can make good use of your own Scrap User's System.

MATERIALS

Yardage is based on 40″ wide fabric

Pink scraps: 2⅜ yards total for blocks and pieced border

Light neutral scraps: 4½ yards total for blocks and pieced borders

Green scraps: 1 yard total for blocks and pieced borders

Raspberry print: ½ yard for border 3

Green print: 1⅜ yards for border 4

Pink print: ⅝ yard for binding

Backing: 7¾ yards

Batting: 92″ × 92″

CUTTING

From pink scraps, cut:
388 squares 2⅜″ × 2⅜″
60 squares 3½″ × 3½″

From light neutral scraps, cut:
388 squares 2⅜″ × 2⅜″
244 squares 2″ × 2″
376 rectangles 2″ × 3½″

From green scraps, cut:
292 squares 2″ × 2″

From raspberry print, cut:
8 strips 1½″ × width of fabric

From green print, cut:
8 strips 5″ × width of fabric

From pink print, cut:
9 binding strips 2″ × width of fabric

Half-Square Triangle Units

A Layer a pink 2⅜″ × 2⅜″ square with a light 2⅜″ × 2⅜″ square, right sides together. Cut on the diagonal from corner to corner to yield 2 half-square triangle pairs. Stitch along the diagonal edge. Press the seams toward the pink fabric. The units will measure 2″ × 2″ and finish 1½″ × 1½″ in the block.

Make a total of 776 pink/light half-square triangle units: use 244 in the Twirl Around blocks; reserve 240 for the alternate blocks and 48 for pieced border 1.

Twirl Around Blocks

While Twirl Around blocks can be assembled in rows, it's easier to keep things spinning in the right direction if you assemble the block in quarters.

B Lay out 1 green 2″ × 2″ square, 1 light 2″ × 2″ square, and 2 half-square triangle units as shown. Stitch into pairs and press; join the pairs to complete the quarter-block. Press the seams in a circular manner to evenly distribute bulk. If all the quarter-blocks are pressed in the same direction, they will nest easily when the block is assembled. If you are consistent in how you sew the quarter-blocks together, the pressing will be the same as well. The units will measure 3½″ × 3½″ and finish 3″ × 3″ in the block. Make 244.

C Lay out 4 quarter-blocks as shown, rotating the units so that the green squares are in the outer block corners.

Sew the quarter-blocks into rows, joining rows to complete each block. Seams where a lot of points come together are sometimes best dealt with by pressing the bulky seams open. The blocks will measure 6½″ × 6½″ and finish 6″ × 6″ in the quilt. Make 61.

Alternate Blocks

I did not strip piece the center section of this block, preferring to use scraps. I assembled my blocks one at a time for the most variety possible. Look at your fabric and determine the best method to get the job done.

D Sew a half-square triangle unit on each end of a light 2″ × 3½″ rectangle. Press the seams toward the rectangle. Make 144.

Set aside 24 of these units for the pieced border.

E Sew a light 2″ × 3½″ rectangle to the opposite sides of a pink 3½″ × 3½″ square to make the center unit. Press the seams toward the rectangles.

F Sew a unit from D to the top and bottom of the center unit. Press the seams toward the center square. The block will measure 6½″ × 6½″ and will finish at 6″ × 6″ in the quilt. Make 60.

Pieced Borders

The pieced borders will complete the design in the center of the quilt.

G   Sew a green 2″ ×2″ square to each end of a light 2″ × 3½″ rectangle. Press toward the squares. Make 20 units.

To make pieced border 1, alternate and sew together 6 of the reserved D units with 5 units from G. Press the seams toward the green squares. Make 4 of these borders.

To make pieced border 2, join 23 light 2″ × 3½″ rectangles end to end. Press the seams in the opposite direction of pieced border 1 so they will nest together when joined. Make 4.

The second pieced border will allow the central design to float and give the eyes a rest.

Quilt Assembly

Lay out the 61 Twirl Around blocks with the 60 alternate blocks in 11 rows of 11 blocks each as shown in the quilt assembly diagram.

Join the blocks into rows. Press seams in opposing directions from row to row. Join the rows to complete the quilt center.

Pieced Borders 1 and 2

Sew a pieced border 1 to opposite sides of the quilt, pinning to match centers and ends. Ease where necessary to fit. Press the seams toward the border.

Add a green 2″ × 2″ square to each end of the top and bottom border 1. Press the seams toward the green squares.

Sew the borders to the quilt top and bottom, pinning to match centers and ends. Ease where necessary to fit. Press the seams toward the borders.

Sew a pieced border 2 to opposite sides of the quilt, pinning to match centers and ends. Ease where necessary to fit. Press the seams toward the border.

Add a green 2″ × 2″ square to each end of the top and bottom border 2. Press the seams toward the light rectangles.

Sew the borders to the quilt top and bottom as before. Press the seams toward the borders.

Border 3

Join the 8 raspberry border strips end to end with diagonal seams to make 1 long strip. Trim the excess fabric ¼″ beyond the stitching; press the seams open.

Lay the quilt center on the floor, smoothing it gently; do not tug or pull. Measure the quilt through the center from top to bottom. Cut side borders to this length. Sew the side borders to the quilt sides, pinning to match centers and ends. Ease where necessary to fit. Press the seams toward the borders.

Repeat for the top and bottom borders, measuring across the quilt center and including the borders just added in the measurement.

Border 4

Join the 8 green border strips end to end with a straight seam to make 1 long strip. Press the seams open.

Repeat the process to measure, cut, and add the green borders to the quilt as before.

Finishing

Layer, quilt, and bind as desired.

I machine quilted *Twirl Around* using a pastel variegated thread in an edge-to-edge design called *Pinwheel #4* by Patricia E. Ritter of Urban Elementz.

I cut binding strips 2″ wide and sew them to the quilt with a ¼″ seam. This gives me a ¼″ finished binding.

Detail of pieced backing

AT A GLANCE

Half-square triangle unit

2″ × 2″ unfinished

Make 776.

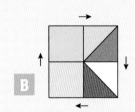
Quarter-block

3½″ × 3½″ unfinished

Make 244.

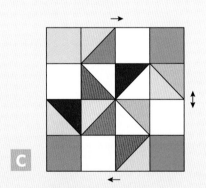
Twirl Around block

6½″ × 6½″ unfinished

Make 61.

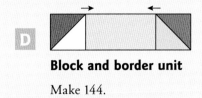
Block and border unit

Make 144.

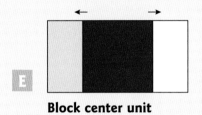
Block center unit

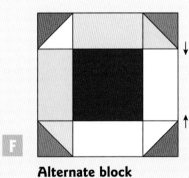
Alternate block

6½″ × 6½″ unfinished

Make 60.

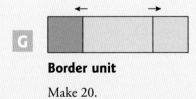
Border unit

Make 20.

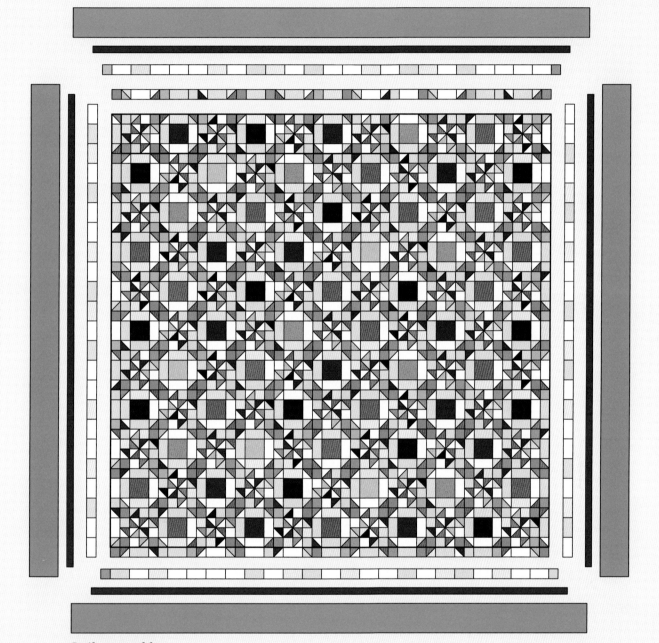

Quilt assembly

Wanderlust

Finished block size: 12″ × 12″ • **Finished quilt:** 74½″ × 86½″

MATERIALS

Yardage is based on 40"-wide fabric.

Medium to dark batik and print scraps: 4½ yards total for blocks and pieced border

Light neutral scraps: 4¼ yards total for blocks and pieced border

Gold, orange, and red scraps: 1¼ yards total for large star points

Black tone-on-tone print: 2¼ yards for blocks and pieced border

Orange batik: ½ yard for inner border

Purple batik: ¾ yard for binding

Backing: 7 yards

Batting: 83" × 95"

HINT Be sure to read this pattern thoroughly and review the piecing diagrams in At A Glance (page 66) before cutting your fabric. Many of the half-square triangles and flying geese units are made in sets of 4 matching units per block. In the small center star, the 4 rectangles used for the flying geese are a different light neutral fabric than the 4 corner squares. Mix and match as you like!

I suggest cutting out pieces for one block at a time and pinning them together in sets before sewing. A small design board covered with flannel is helpful for keeping things in order at the machine.

CUTTING

For 1 Block

Cut a total of 28. Totals are included for the black tone-on-tone if you want to cut the pieces for all the blocks at once.

From medium to dark scraps, cut:	*From light neutral scraps, cut:*
1 square 2½" × 2½"	4 matching 1½" × 2½" rectangles
8 matching squares 1½" × 1½"	4 matching 1½" × 1½" squares
4 matching sets of 2 squares 2⅞" × 2⅞" and 2 squares 2½" × 2½"	4 sets of 2 matching squares 2⅞" × 2⅞"
	4 matching rectangles 2½" × 4½"

From gold, orange, or red scraps, cut:	*From black tone-on-tone, cut:*
8 matching 2½" × 2½" squares	4 rectangles 2½" × 4½" (112 total)

Cutting continued on next page.

I had originally planned on setting these blocks in a straight set with sashing and cornerstones. However, with the help of my dog, Sadie, and her inadvertently rearranging them on my "design floor" while I wasn't looking, I discovered how fun the secondary design was if I dropped every other row by half a block. Yes, my quilting has gone to the dogs, and it is all the better for it!

Many of the batiks in this quilt were brought home from a trip to Bali, and I was happy to have a place for them to land. I freely mixed my batiks with regular cotton prints and recycled fabrics from men's shirts, along with a black print for my own eclectic combination.

I also used two sizes of strips from my Scrap User's System (page 7)—1½" and 2½" strips worked up easily into the flying geese and half-square triangles, thanks to my Essential Triangle Tool.

Traditional rotary cutting measurements are given; modify them as needed for specialty tools. Know your tools and they can save you time.

You can use any method for flying geese and half-square triangles that gives you the required size of unit.

Cutting continued.

For 1 Half-Block

Cut a total of 4. Totals are included for the black tone-on-tone if you want to cut the pieces for all the blocks at once.

From medium to dark scraps, cut:

1 rectangle 1½″ × 2½″

1 matching set of 2 squares 1½″ × 1½″ and 1 square 1⅞″ × 1⅞″

2 matching sets of 3 squares 2⅞″ × 2⅞″ and 1 square 2½″ × 2½″

From light neutral scraps, cut:

1 rectangle 1½″ × 2½″ and 1 matching square 1⅞″ × 1⅞″

2 matching squares 1½″ × 1½″

1 rectangle 2½″ × 4½″ and 1 matching square 2⅞″ × 2⅞″

2 sets of 2 matching squares 2⅞″ × 2⅞″

From gold, orange, or red scraps, cut:

1 matching set of 2 squares 2½″ × 2½″ and 1 square 2⅞″ × 2⅞″

From black tone-on-tone, cut:

1 rectangle 2½″ × 4½″ (4 total)

1 square 2⅞″ × 2⅞″ (4 total)

Borders and Binding

From orange batik, cut:

8 strips 1½″ × width of fabric

4 rectangles 1½″ × 6½″

From medium to dark scraps, cut:

48 sets of 3 matching squares 2⅞″ × 2⅞″

From light neutral scraps, cut:

48 sets of 2 matching squares 2⅞″ × 2⅞″

From black tone-on-tone, cut:

5 strips 6⅞″ × width of fabric; subcut into:

24 squares 6⅞″ × 6⅞″; cut diagonally once to yield 48 triangles

From purple batik, cut:

9 binding strips 2″ × width of fabric

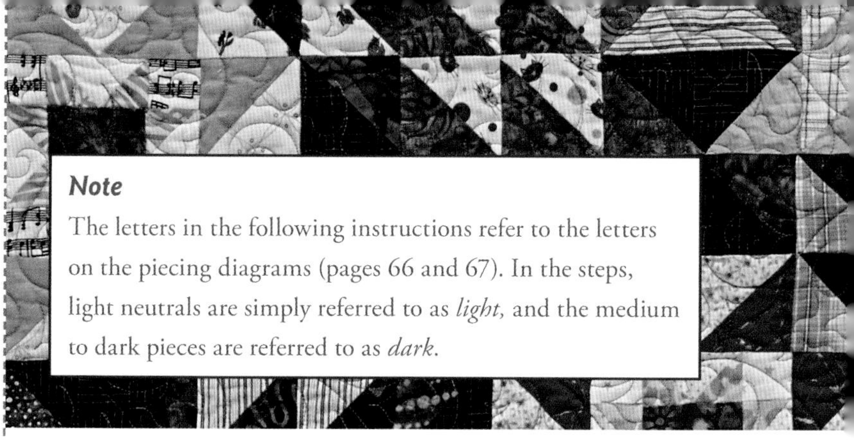

> **Note**
> The letters in the following instructions refer to the letters on the piecing diagrams (pages 66 and 67). In the steps, light neutrals are simply referred to as *light,* and the medium to dark pieces are referred to as *dark*.

Wanderlust Blocks

Because the half-square triangle units in the corners of the block determine the colors of the adjacent flying geese, you'll make the outer flying geese *last* so it's easy to determine what color goes where.

Block Centers

Draw a line from corner to corner on the wrong side of 8 matching 1½″ × 1½″ dark squares.

A   Pair a marked square with a light 1½″ × 2½″ rectangle as shown. Stitch with the needle kissing up to the drawn line. Trim the excess fabric ¼″ from the stitching. Press the seam toward the triangle.

HINT *Do not sew right on the line!* The line is your *fold* line, not your stitching line. Set the needle just to the right of the line, toward the outer corner of the unit. This way the line will fold up and end up right on top of your thread where it belongs, and the edge of your stitch-and-flip corner will reach the rectangle's outer edges.

B   Repeat with a second square on the opposite end of the rectangle. Make 4 matching flying geese units for the center star. The flying geese will measure 1½″ × 2½″ and finish 1″ × 2″ in the block.

C   Arrange the 4 flying geese units, 1 dark 2½″ × 2½″ square, and 4 matching light 1½″ × 1½″ squares as shown. Stitch the units into rows and join the rows to complete the star for the block center. Press.

Block Corners

D Layer 2 matching dark 2⅞″ × 2⅞″ squares with 2 matching light 2⅞″ × 2⅞″ squares, right sides together. Cut from corner to corner once on the diagonal to yield 4 matching triangle pairs. Stitch and press toward the dark fabric. Trim the dog-ears.

Repeat to make a total of 4 sets of 4 matching half-square triangle units for 1 block. Set aside the matching 2½″ × 2½″ squares to make the outer flying geese units later.

E Lay out 4 matching half-square triangle units as shown, joining units into rows. Join the rows to complete the block corner unit. Press the seams open. Make 4 for 1 block.

> **Note**
> I pressed several seam allowances open in these blocks because it's not always possible to press so the seams will nest. Use your best judgment and press open when needed to minimize bulk. Pressing solely toward the dark is not a hard-and-fast rule.

Large Star Points

Draw a diagonal line from corner to corner on the wrong side of 8 matching gold, orange, or red 2½″ × 2½″ squares for the large star points.

F Choose a set of 4 matching light 2½″ × 4½″ rectangles. Pair the marked squares with the rectangles and sew as before to make flying geese units. Make 4 matching flying geese units for 1 block.

Remember to stitch to the *right* of the drawn line, with the stitching falling toward the corner that will be trimmed. Fold the triangle over on the stitching line to double-check that it reaches the outside edge of the base rectangle. Trim the excess fabric ¼″ beyond the stitching. Repeat for the remaining side of the unit.

Block Assembly

G Lay out the block center, corner units, large star points, and 4 black 2½″ × 4½″ rectangles.

Place the matching 2½″ × 2½″ squares (set aside earlier) with the black rectangles so that the colors match the adjacent corner units. Draw a diagonal line from corner to corner on the wrong side of the squares and sew them to the rectangles as you did for the flying geese units. Press the seams toward the corner triangles. Make 4 for the block.

H Join the black flying geese units to the large star point units as shown. Press the seams open to minimize bulk.

I Sew the units into rows and then sew the rows together to complete the block. Each block will measure 12½″ × 12½″ and will finish 12″ × 12″ in the quilt.

Repeat the steps to make a total of 28 blocks.

Wanderlust Half-Blocks

Half-Star

Draw a diagonal line from corner to corner on the wrong side of 2 matching dark 1½″ × 1½″ squares. Pair the marked squares with a light 1½″ × 2½″ rectangle and make a flying geese unit as before.

Layer the matching dark 1⅞″ × 1⅞″ square with the matching light 1⅞″ × 1⅞″ square, right sides together. Cut once on the diagonal from corner to corner. Sew together along the diagonal to make 2 half-square triangle units. Press the seams toward the dark triangle and trim the dog-ears.

J Arrange the 2 half-square triangle units, the flying geese unit, a dark 1½″ × 2½″ rectangle, and 2 light 1½″ × 1½″ squares as shown. Stitch the units into rows and join the rows to complete the half-star. Press.

Block Corners

Repeat the steps under Block Corners (page 63) to make 2 sets of 4 matching half-square triangle units for a half-block. Sew them together to make 2 block corner units.

Set aside the matching 2½″ × 2½″ squares for the outer flying geese units.

Layer the remaining 2⅞″ × 2⅞″ square of each fabric with a black 2⅞″ × 2⅞″ square. Cut once on the diagonal from corner to corner. Sew together along the diagonal to make 2 half-square triangle units of each color. Press the seams toward the black triangle and trim the dog-ears. You'll use only one of each of these units in the block. Save the remaining units for another project.

Large Star Points

Draw a diagonal line from corner to corner on the wrong side of 2 matching gold, orange, or red 2½″ × 2½″ squares for the large star points.

Pair the marked squares with a light 2½″ × 4½″ rectangle and sew as before to make a flying geese unit.

Layer the matching gold, orange, or red 2⅞″ × 2⅞″ square with the matching light 2⅞″ × 2⅞″ square, right sides together. Cut once on the diagonal from corner to corner. Sew along the diagonal to make 2 half-square triangle units. Press the seams toward the dark triangle and trim the dog-ears.

Half-Block Assembly

Lay out the half-star, corner units, half-square triangle units, flying geese unit, and a black 2½″ × 4½″ rectangle.

Place the matching 2½″ × 2½″ squares (set aside earlier) with the black rectangle so that the colors match the adjacent corner units. Draw a diagonal line from corner to corner on the wrong side of the squares and sew them to the rectangle as you did for the flying geese unit. Press the seams toward the corner triangles.

Join the black flying geese unit to the large star point unit. Press the seams open to minimize bulk.

K Sew the units into rows; then sew the rows together to complete the half-block. Each half-block will measure 12½″ × 6½″ and will finish 12″ × 6″ in the quilt.

L Repeat the steps to make a total of 4 half-blocks.

Quilt Assembly

This is a design floor process for me. I arrange and rearrange until I am happy with the layout. In this case, I had help from my dog.

Refer to the quilt assembly diagram to lay out the blocks in 5 vertical columns: Columns 1, 3, and 5 will have 6 blocks. Columns 2 and 4 start and end with half-blocks, with 5 blocks in between. Join the blocks into columns. Press seams in opposing directions from column to column. Join the columns to complete the quilt center. Press.

Borders

Border Blocks

Layer 2 matching dark 2⅞″ × 2⅞″ squares with 2 matching light 2⅞″ × 2⅞″ squares, right sides together. Place another matching dark square on top of the set. You will be cutting through 5 layers.

Cut the set on the diagonal from corner to corner once to yield 4 matched triangle pairs and 1 pair of dark triangles. Save one of the light triangles for another project.

Stitch the remaining matched triangle pairs along the diagonal to make 3 half-square triangle units. Press the seams toward the dark triangle and trim the dog-ears.

M Lay out the triangles and half-square triangle units as shown; pair with a black triangle. Join the units into rows and join the rows. Sew the pieced triangle to the black triangle to complete the pieced border block. Press the seam toward the black triangle. The block will measure 6½″ × 6½″ and finish 6″ × 6″ in the quilt.

N Repeat the steps to make a total of 48 border blocks.

Border Assembly

Sew the 8 orange inner border strips together, end to end and on the diagonal. Trim the excess fabric ¼″ away from the stitching and press the seams open. Cut 2 lengths at 72½″ for the sides and 2 lengths at 74½″ for the top and bottom.

O Join 12 border blocks as shown. Press. Make 2 for the quilt sides.

Sew the 72½″ orange borders to the side borders as shown, matching centers and ends. Press seams toward the orange border.

Add the borders to the quilt sides, pinning centers and ends and easing where necessary to fit. Press seams toward the orange border.

P Sew 10 border blocks together; stitch an orange 1½″ × 6½″ rectangle to each end. Add a border block to each end, pressing toward the orange rectangles. Stitch an orange 74½″ strip to the top of the border. Make 2 for the top and bottom of the quilt.

Sew the borders to the top and bottom of the quilt, matching centers and ends. Press toward the orange border.

Finishing

Layer, quilt, and bind as desired.

I quilted *Wanderlust* with a dark gold thread in an edge-to-edge design called *Dusty Miller—Grande* by Patricia E. Ritter of Urban Elementz.

I cut binding strips 2″ wide and sew the binding to the quilt with a ¼″ seam. This gives me a ¼″ finished binding that doesn't nip off the points of the patchwork units.

AT A GLANCE

Flying geese construction

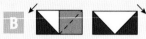

Small flying geese unit

Make 4 per block.

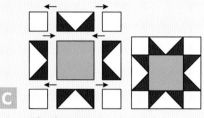

Block center

4½″ × 4½″ unfinished

Half-square triangle units

Make 4 sets of 4 per block.

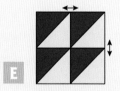

Block corner

4½″ × 4½″ unfinished

Make 4 per block.

Large star point

Make 4 per block.

Block layout

Determine flying geese colors.

Unit assembly

Make 4 per block.

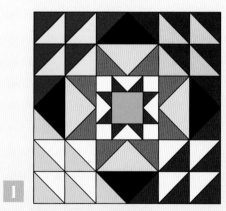

Wanderlust block

12½″ × 12½″ unfinished

Make 28.

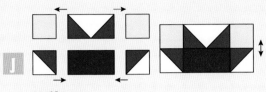

J

Half-star

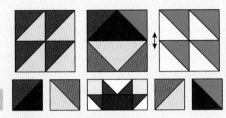

K

Half-block assembly

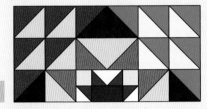

L

Half-block

12½″ × 6½″ unfinished

Make 4.

M

Border block assembly

N

Border block

6½″ × 6½″ unfinished

Make 48.

O

Side border

Make 2.

P

Top and bottom border

Make 2.

Quilt assembly

Box Kite

Finished block size: 6" × 6" • Finished quilt: 72½" × 84½"

MATERIALS

Yardage is based on 40"-wide fabric.

Medium to dark scraps: 4 yards total for blocks

Light neutral scraps: 4½ yards total for blocks and border

Red print: ⅔ yard for inner border

Black print: ¾ yard for binding

Backing: 5¼ yards

Batting: 81" × 93"

HINT It's helpful to read this pattern and study the diagrams thoroughly before cutting your fabric. The half-square triangle units for the blocks are made in sets of 6 matching units per block. I cut each block individually and pinned the pieces for each block together before sewing. Within each block, all the lights are the same fabric. The center square is different from the dark scraps used in the half-square triangle units.

CUTTING

For 1 Block

Cut a total of 120.

From medium to dark scraps, cut:

3 matching squares 2⅞" × 2⅞"

1 square 2½" × 2½"

From light neutral scraps, cut:

1 matching set of 3 squares 2⅞" × 2⅞" and 2 squares 2½" × 2½"

Borders and Binding

From medium to dark scraps, cut:

38 squares 5¼" × 5¼"

From light neutral scraps, cut:

36 squares 5¼" × 5¼"

From red print, cut:

8 strips 2½" × width of fabric

From black print, cut:

9 binding strips 2" × width of fabric.

I love half-square triangles! I love simple blocks with half-square triangles. The designs and layouts and ideas are endless. This design uses the traditional Box Kite block in a 6" finished size, allowing for loads of repeat across the quilt and letting all these triangles sparkle.

Triangles are exceptionally quick and easy when cut from pairs of strips that are layered right sides together. I can use strips from my Scrap User's System to cut them from standard strip widths without worrying about the extra ⅜" when using specialty triangle rulers such as my Essential Triangle Tool.

The outer border is the perfect frame for all the triangle patchwork. The larger quarter-square triangles are easily cut from the same size strips as the Box Kite blocks, using the same triangle ruler. It makes the job quick, fun, and easy.

Traditional rotary cutting measurements are given; modify them as needed for specialty tools. Know your tools and use them to your advantage.

You can use any method for flying geese and half-square triangles that give you the required size of unit.

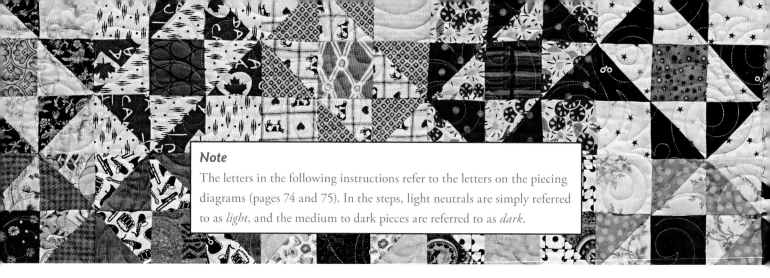

Blocks

A Layer 3 matching dark 2⅞″ × 2⅞″ squares with 3 matching light 2⅞″ × 2⅞″ squares, right sides together. Cut on the diagonal from corner to corner once to yield 6 matched half-square triangle pairs. Stitch the pairs along the diagonal. Press toward the dark and trim the dog-ears. The units should measure 2½″ × 2½″ and finish 2″ × 2″ in the quilt.

B Lay out the half-square triangle units, 2 matching light 2½″ × 2½″ squares, and a dark 2½″ × 2½″ square as shown. Stitch the units into rows and press. Join the rows to complete the block. Press.

C Repeat the steps to make 120 Box Kite blocks.

Quilt Assembly

Lay out the blocks as shown in the quilt assembly diagram, with 10 blocks across and 12 blocks down. Join the blocks into rows; press seam allowances in opposing directions from row to row. Join the rows to complete the quilt center. Press.

Inner Border

Join the 8 red print strips end to end with diagonal seams to make 1 long strip. Trim the excess fabric ¼″ beyond the stitching and press the seams open.

Lay the quilt center on the floor, smoothing it gently; do not tug or pull. Measure the quilt through the center from top to bottom. Cut side borders this length. Sew the side borders to the quilt sides, with right sides together and pinning to match centers and ends. Ease where necessary to fit. Press the seams toward the borders.

Measure across the quilt center, including the borders just added in the measurement. Cut the top and bottom borders to this length. Stitch them to the quilt center, pinning to match centers and ends; ease where necessary to fit. Press the seams toward the borders.

Pieced Outer Border

> **Note**
> The border units are cut as quarter-square triangles so that the edges of the borders will be on the straight of grain.

Layer 19 dark 5¼″ × 5¼″ squares with 19 light 5¼″ × 5¼″ squares, right sides together. Cut through each pair on the diagonal twice to yield 76 pairs of quarter-square triangles.

D Stitch a triangle pair along the diagonal straight-grain side to make a pieced border square. Carefully press the seams toward the dark, as the outer edges are bias. Make 74. You'll have 2 extra pairs; set them aside for the next step.

Cut the remaining 17 light 5¼″ × 5¼″ squares and the remaining 19 dark 5¼″ × 5¼″ squares twice on the diagonal to yield 68 light and 76 dark quarter-square triangles. Add the set-aside triangles to this group.

E Sew a light triangle to the left of a pieced border square and sew a dark triangle to the right as shown. Press the seams toward the triangles just added. Make 62 border units.

F Add 2 light triangles to the dark sides of a half-square triangle unit as shown. Press the seams toward the light triangles. Make 4 of these end units.

G Add 2 dark triangles to the light sides of a half-square triangle unit as shown. Wait until the next step to press the seams. Make 8.

H Pair 2 of the G units to make a border corner as shown. Press the seams so they will nest; then sew together. Press the seams to one side. Make 4.

I Join 17 border units side by side as shown. Press. Add a border end unit to the right side, creating a trapezoid side border. Make 2.

J Join 14 border units side by side as shown. Press. Add a border end unit to the right side, creating a trapezoid top and bottom border. Make 2.

Join the side borders to the quilt, pinning to match centers and ends and overlapping the dog-ears of the pieced border ¼″ beyond the red inner border at each end. Ease where necessary to fit. Stitch. Repeat for the opposite side border. Press the seams toward the inner border.

Join the top and bottom borders to the quilt as before. Press toward the inner border.

Add the pieced border corners to the quilt to complete the pieced outer border. Press.

Finishing

Layer, quilt, and bind as desired.

I quilted *Box Kite* using gold thread with an edge-to-edge design called *Plume* by Hermione Agee of Lorien Quilting.

A double-fold black binding finishes the quilt. I cut strips 2″ wide and sew the binding to the quilt with a ¼″ seam. This gives me a ¼″ finished binding and doesn't nip off the corners of the patchwork units.

AT A GLANCE

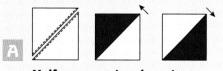

A

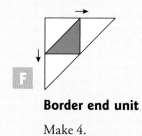

F

Border end unit

Make 4.

Half-square triangle units

2½″ × 2½″ unfinished

Make 6 matching sets per block.

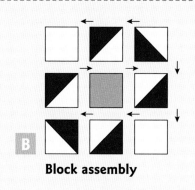

B

Block assembly

G

Border corner unit

Make 8.

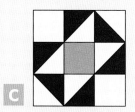

C

Box Kite block

6½″ × 6½″ unfinished

Make 120.

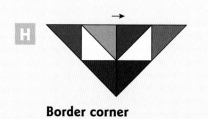

H

Border corner

Make 4.

D

Pieced border square

Make 74.

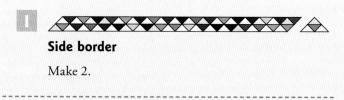

I

Side border

Make 2.

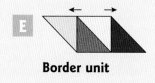

E

Border unit

Make 62.

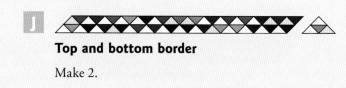

J

Top and bottom border

Make 2.

Quilt assembly

Garden Party

Finished block size: 5" × 5" • Finished quilt: 82" × 82"

MATERIALS

Medium to dark scraps: 3 yards total for Garden Posey block

Red scraps: 1⅔ yards total for Garden Chain block and setting triangles

Light neutral scraps: 3¼ yards total for both blocks

Cream polka dot: ½ yard for inner border

Red floral print: 1¼ yards for outer border

Turquoise plaid: ¾ yard for binding

Backing: 7¾ yards

Batting: 90″ × 90″

This quilt was designed to use small treasured scraps of fabric. No two blocks look alike. I found it helpful to cut each Garden Posey block individually, pinning parts for each block in sets before sewing. Or you can cut all the pieces at once and then have fun combining them as you go.

Be bold! Be brilliant, go out of the box, and play with color combinations you may never have thought of before!

CUTTING

Garden Posey Blocks

From medium to dark scraps, cut:

100 matching sets of 1 rectangle 1½″ × 6½″ and 4 rectangles 1½″ × 2½″

100 sets of 4 matching rectangles 1½″ × 2½″

100 squares 1½″ × 1½″

From light neutral scraps, cut:

100 rectangles 1½″ × 6½″

Garden Chain Blocks

From red scraps, cut:

30–40 strips 1½″ wide in random lengths*

From light neutral scraps, cut:

15–20 strips 1½″ wide in random lengths*

15–20 strips 3½″ wide in random lengths*

198 rectangles 1½″ × 3½″

Setting Triangles, Borders, and Binding

From red scraps, cut:

76 squares 1½″ × 1½″

15–20 strips 1½″ wide in random lengths*

From light neutral scraps, cut:

15–20 strips 1½″ wide in random lengths*

From cream polka dot, cut:

8 strips 1½″ × width of fabric

From red floral print, cut:

8 strips 5″ × width of fabric

From turquoise plaid, cut:

9 binding strips 2″ × width of fabric

Cut more strips as needed when sewing strip sets to obtain the required number of segments.

I like playing with color and patterns that repeat. Small blocks are a favorite, and the more repeats across the quilt surface, the more interesting the pattern becomes. This quilt reminds me so much of my mother's beautiful garden in Garden Valley, Idaho. Meticulously cared for, flowers bloom continuously through the summer months, separated by garden paths for walking, reflecting, and enjoying.

All the pieces for the main blocks and for the framed nine-patch alternate blocks came from my burgeoning 1½″ strip stash in my Scrap User's System. Some 3½″ strips were also used in the strip sets that frame the nine patches—it's a scrap user's dream quilt!

The best part of this quilt? No triangles to sew!

Garden Posey Blocks

A Sew a light 1½″ × 6½″ rectangle to a dark 1½″ × 6½″ rectangle along one long side with a ¼″ seam. Press the seam toward the dark strip and measure. The strip set should measure 2½″ tall. If it doesn't, adjust the seam allowance until it does.

Crosscut the strip set into 4 segments 1½″ wide; the ½″ extra allows for squaring and trimming.

B Sew a matching dark 1½″ × 2½″ rectangle to 1 segment as shown. Press the seam toward the rectangle so the seams will nest later. The unit will measure 2½″ × 2½″ and finish 2″ × 2″ in the quilt. Make 4 units for the block corners.

C Lay out 4 block corners, 4 matching dark 1½″ × 2½″ rectangles, and a dark 1½″ × 1½″ square as shown. Join the units into rows; press the seams toward the sashing. Join the rows to complete the block.

D Repeat the steps to make 100 blocks.

Garden Chain Blocks

E Sew a red 1½″ strip to each side of a light 1½″ strip to make strip set E; press the seams toward the red. To get as much variety as possible, sew short strip sets and mix up the fabrics. Crosscut the strip sets into 1½″-wide segments. Cut a total of 202 segments.

F Sew a light 1½″ strip to each side of a red 1½″ strip to make strip set F; press the seams toward the red. Make several and crosscut the strip sets into 1½″-wide segments. Cut a total of 81 segments.

G Sew a segment from F between 2 segments from E to make a nine-patch unit. Make 81. Set aside the remaining 40 segments from E for the pieced setting triangles.

H Sew a red 1½″ strip to each side of a light 3½″ strip to make a strip set. Press the seams toward the red. Make several and crosscut into 1½″-wide segments. Cut a total of 202 segments.

I Sew a light 1½″ × 3½″ rectangle to each side of the nine-patch unit. Press toward the rectangles. Sew a segment from H to the top and bottom of the block, nesting seams. Press the seams away from the center. Make 81 blocks.

Set aside the remaining 40 segments from H for the pieced setting triangles.

Side Setting Triangles

J Sew a red 1½″ strip to a light 1½″ strip to make a strip set. Press toward the red. Make as many as needed to cut 36 two-patch segments 1½″ wide.

K Arrange a reserved segment from E, a two-patch segment from J, and a red 1½″ × 1½″ square as shown. Sew together to make a triangle center. Make 36.

L Sew a red 1½″ × 1½″ square to a light 1½″ × 3½″ rectangle. Press the seams toward the red square to make a sashing unit. Make 36.

M Sew a sashing unit from L to the bottom of the triangle center. Press toward the triangle center. Add a reserved segment from H to the left side and press toward the segment. Make 36.

Corner Setting Triangles

N Sew a red 1½″ × 1½″ square to a reserved segment from E, centering it on the light square. Press toward the square. Join the unit to a reserved segment from H, centering it on the light rectangle. The ends of the three-patch will extend ¼″ beyond the seams of the H unit. Press toward the H segment. Make 4 corner setting triangles.

Quilt Assembly

Refer to the quilt assembly diagram to lay out the blocks in diagonal rows, alternating the Garden Posey blocks and the Garden Chain blocks. Fill in the sides with the side and corner setting triangles.

I like to piece diagonally set quilts in 2 sections and then join the sections. This keeps things from being too unwieldy, especially when sewing a large quilt top.

Starting in a corner, sew the blocks and triangles into diagonal rows. Press seams in opposing directions from row to row. Sew the rows together into 2 sections; press the seams in one direction. Sew the 2 sections together to complete the quilt center. Press.

Trim It Up!

Before trimming, use a long straight stitch to staystitch by machine around the edges of the quilt, just outside the light squares. The red squares will finish as triangles at the edge of the quilt and will be on the bias. The stay stitching helps control any stretching.

Trim the edges of the quilt measuring ¼″ beyond the corners of the light squares. This will give you a seam allowance to add the inner borders without losing the points of the light squares.

Borders

Join the 8 cream polka-dot inner border strips end to end on the diagonal to make 1 long strip. Trim the excess fabric ¼″ from the stitching and press the seams open.

Lay the quilt center on the floor, smoothing it gently; do not tug or pull. Measure the quilt through the center from top to bottom. Cut side inner borders to this length. Sew the side borders to the quilt, pinning to match centers and ends and easing where necessary to fit. Press toward the borders.

Repeat for the top and bottom borders, measuring across the quilt center and including the borders just added in the measurement. Cut the top and bottom borders to this length and sew them to the quilt center, pinning to match centers and ends and easing where necessary to fit. Press toward the borders.

Join the 8 red floral print outer border strips end to end with straight seams to make 1 long strip. Press the seams open.

Add the outer borders in the same manner as the inner borders.

Finishing

Layer, quilt, and bind as desired.

I machine quilted *Garden Party* with tan thread using an edge-to-edge design called *Tailfeathers* by Hermione Agee of Lorien Quilting.

Add the turquoise plaid binding strips for the perfect ending! I cut binding strips 2″ wide and sew them to the quilt with a ¼″ seam. This gives me a ¼″ finished binding.

AT A GLANCE

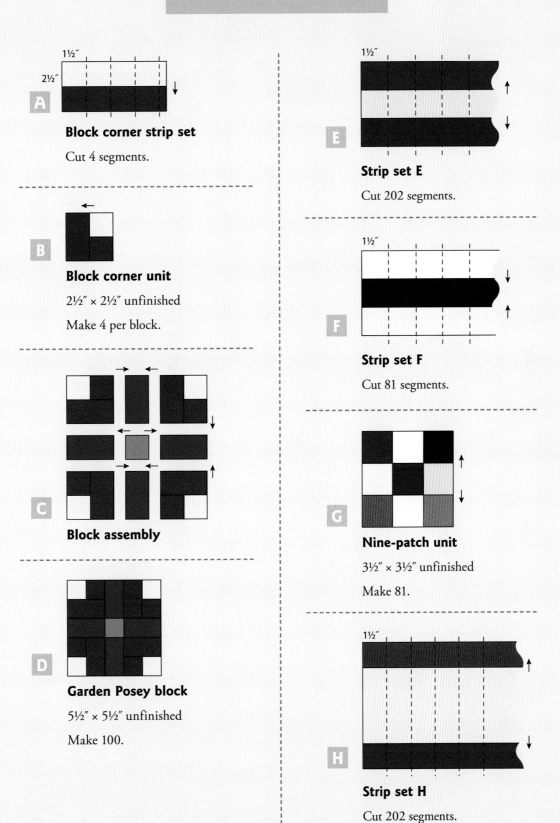

A

Block corner strip set

Cut 4 segments.

1½″   2½″

B

Block corner unit

2½″ × 2½″ unfinished

Make 4 per block.

C

Block assembly

D

Garden Posey block

5½″ × 5½″ unfinished

Make 100.

E

Strip set E

Cut 202 segments.

1½″

F

Strip set F

Cut 81 segments.

1½″

G

Nine-patch unit

3½″ × 3½″ unfinished

Make 81.

H

Strip set H

Cut 202 segments.

1½″

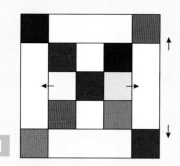

Garden Chain block

5½″ × 5½″ unfinished

Make 81.

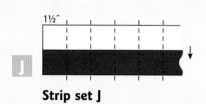

Strip set J

Cut 36 segments.

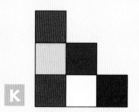

Triangle center

Make 36.

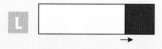

Sashing unit

Make 36.

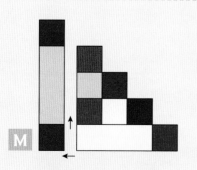

Side setting triangle

Make 36.

Corner setting triangle

Make 4.

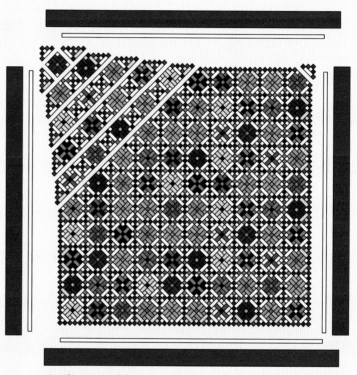

Quilt assembly

Tropical Twist

Finished block size: 12″ × 12″ • **Finished quilt:** 80½″ × 92½″

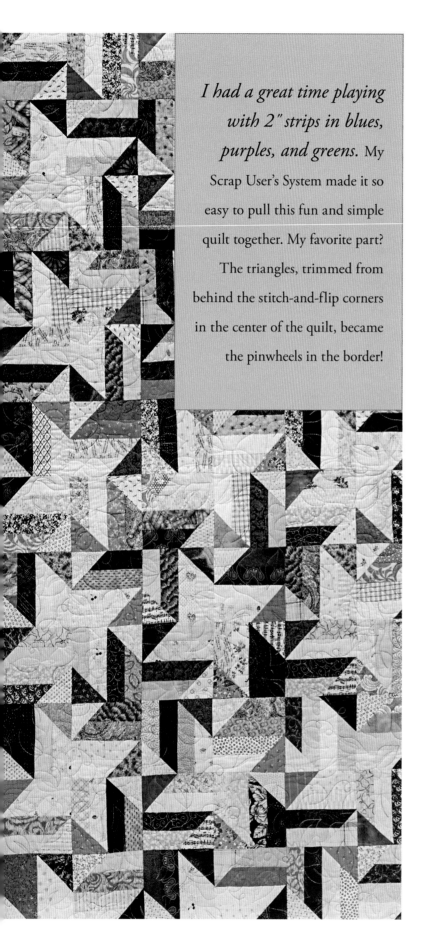

I had a great time playing with 2" strips in blues, purples, and greens. My Scrap User's System made it so easy to pull this fun and simple quilt together. My favorite part? The triangles, trimmed from behind the stitch-and-flip corners in the center of the quilt, became the pinwheels in the border!

MATERIALS

Yardage is based on 40"-wide fabric.

Medium, dark blue, and green scraps: 3½ yards total for blocks

Light scraps: 3½ yards total for blocks

Teal tone-on-tone: ⅝ yard for inner border 1

Yellow print: ½ yard for inner border 2

Purple tone-on-tone: 1 yard for outer border

Purple print: ¾ yard for binding

Backing: 7½ yards

Batting: 89" × 101"

CUTTING

Blocks

From medium, dark blue, and green scraps, cut:

40 strips 2" × width of fabric

120 squares 3½" × 3½"

From light scraps, cut:

40 strips 2" × width of fabric

120 squares 3½" × 3½"

Borders and Binding

From teal tone-on-tone, cut:

8 strips 2" × width of fabric

From yellow print, cut:

8 strips 1½" × width of fabric

From purple tone-on-tone, cut:

5 strips 5½" × width of fabric; subcut:

  56 rectangles 3" × 5½"

  4 rectangles 1½" × 5½"

4 rectangles 3" × 8"

From purple print, cut:

10 binding strips 2" × width of fabric

Tropical Twist Blocks

A Randomly sew pairs of light 2″ strips together to make a strip set. Make 20 strip sets. Cut the strips at 6½″ intervals to make 120 light segments. Repeat with the dark strips to make 120 dark segments.

B **C** Place a dark 3½″ × 3½″ square on the right end of a light segment, right sides together. Draw a diagonal line from corner to corner on the square as shown. Draw another line ⅜″ away, closer to the outer corner. Sew on both lines. Cut between the sewn lines. Flip the triangle open and press toward the corner of the light segment; press the seam of the half-square triangle toward the unpieced triangle.

The half-square triangles will measure 3″ × 3″ and finish 2½″ × 2½″ in the border. Make 120 of each unit.

D **E** Repeat the steps with the dark segments and light 3½″ × 3½″ squares. Make 120 of each unit.

F Sew a light rectangle unit and a dark rectangle unit together as shown. Press. Make 4 of these units per block for 120 total.

G Sew the units together in pairs and join the pairs to make a block. The block will measure 12½″ × 12½″ and finish 12″ × 12″ in the quilt. Make 30 blocks.

Quilt Assembly

Lay out the blocks in 6 rows of 5 blocks each. Join the blocks in rows; press seams in opposing directions from row to row. Join the rows and press the seams in one direction.

Borders

Inner Borders

Join the 8 teal inner border strips (2″ wide) end to end with diagonal seams to make 1 long strip. Trim the excess fabric ¼″ beyond the stitching, and press the seams open.

Lay the quilt center on the floor, smoothing it gently; do not tug or pull. Measure the quilt through the center from top to bottom. Cut side borders this length. Sew the side borders to the quilt sides with right sides together, pinning to match centers and ends. Ease where necessary to fit. Press the seams toward the borders.

Repeat for the top and bottom borders, measuring across the quilt center and including the borders just added in the measurement.

Join the 8 yellow print inner border strips (1½″ wide) end to end with diagonal seams to make 1 long strip. Trim the excess fabric ¼″ beyond the stitching, and press the seams open.

Repeat the process to measure, cut, and add the yellow inner borders.

Measure the quilt through the center from top to bottom and take note of this measurement.

Outer Border Blocks

H Sew 4 similar half-square triangles together in pairs. Press. Join the pairs to make a Pinwheel block. The blocks will measure 5½″ × 5½″ and finish 5″ × 5″ in the quilt. Make 60.

I Sew a purple 3″ × 5½″ rectangle to the bottom of a Pinwheel block. Press toward the rectangle. Sew a purple 3″ × 8″ rectangle to the left side to make a corner block. Make 4.

J Sew a purple 3″ × 5½″ rectangle to each of the remaining Pinwheel blocks to make border units. Press toward the rectangle. Make 56.

Add Borders

Sew 15 border units together as shown in the quilt assembly diagram to make a side border. Add a purple 1½″ × 5½″ rectangle to each end of the border. Make 2.

The added rectangles will allow you to adjust the length of the border to your quilt measurement. I managed to get my borders to fit without them, but measure your quilt as you did for the inner borders and adjust the length as needed. Sew the borders to the sides of the quilt top. Press the seams toward the inner border.

Sew 13 border units together as shown. Sew a corner block to each end. Sew to the top and bottom of the quilt. Press the seams toward the inner border.

Finishing

Layer, quilt, and bind as desired.

I machine quilted *Tropical Twist* using a pastel variegated thread, stitching freehand leaves and loops to create tendrils.

A purple print in a striped pattern created the perfect binding. I cut binding strips 2″ wide and sew the binding to the quilt with a ¼″ finished binding that doesn't nip off the points of the patchwork units.

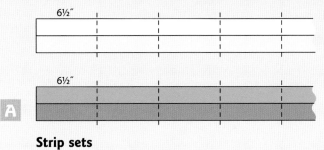

A

Strip sets

Cut 120 segments from each.

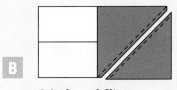

B

Stitch and flip

Sew on both lines and cut.

C

Light units

Make 120 of each.

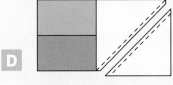

D

Stitch and flip

Sew on both lines and cut.

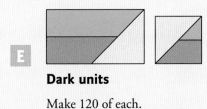

E

Dark units

Make 120 of each.

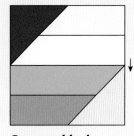

F

Quarter-block

Make 120.

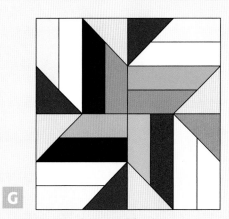

G

Tropical Twist block

12½″ × 12½″ unfinished

Make 30.

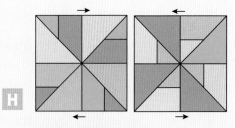

H

Border pinwheels

Make 60 total.

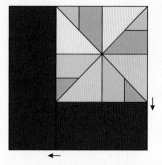

Border corner block

Make 4.

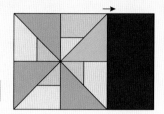

Pinwheel border unit

Make 56.

Quilt assembly

Jingle Bell Square

Finished block size: 8" × 8" • Finished quilt: 84½" × 84½"

Christmas fabrics!
Many of us have holiday-themed fabrics dating back years. What can you do with older Christmas prints? Pull them out and let them play! I combined older Christmas prints with newer and brighter updated holiday fabrics for a quilt that blends Christmas Past with Christmas Present.

I used my Essential Triangle Tool with 1½" and 2½" strips from my Scrap User's System to quickly make the hour glass units in the sizes needed for these adorable blocks.

Traditional rotary cutting measurements are given; modify them as needed for specialty tools. Know your tools and have fun with them!

MATERIALS

Yardage is based on 40"-wide fabric.

Red scraps: 3¾ yards total for blocks, cornerstones, borders, and binding

Cream scraps: 2½ yards total for blocks and outer border

Green scraps: 3 yards total for blocks, cornerstones, and borders

Cream tone-on-tone: 2 yards for sashing

Backing: 8 yards

Batting: 92" × 92"

CUTTING

From red scraps, cut:

25 sets of 2 matching squares 3¼" × 3¼"

33 squares 5¼" × 5¼"

49 sets of 4 matching rectangles 1½" × 4½"

40 squares 2½" × 2½"

8 squares 1½" × 1½"

1½" strips in random lengths to total 320" for inner border

2" strips in random lengths to total 360" for binding

From cream scraps, cut:

49 sets of 2 matching squares 3¼" × 3¼"

63 squares 5¼" × 5¼"

From green scraps, cut:

24 sets of 2 matching squares 3¼" × 3¼"

30 squares 5¼" × 5¼"

49 sets of 4 matching rectangles 1½" × 4½"

40 squares 2½" × 2½"

8 squares 1½" × 1½"

1½" strips in random lengths to total 320" for inner border

From cream tone-on-tone, cut:

7 strips 8½" × width of fabric; subcut 112 rectangles 2½" × 8½"

Note

The letters in the following instructions refer to the letters on the piecing diagrams (pages 93 and 94).

Hour Glass Units for Blocks and Border

Layer 2 matching red 3¼″ × 3¼″ squares with 2 matching cream 3¼″ × 3¼″ squares, right sides together. Cut on the diagonal twice to yield 8 pairs of triangles.

A B Sew the pairs together; press seams the toward the red. Sew the units together to make 4 matching hour glass units. The units will measure 2½″ × 2½″ and finish 2″ × 2″ in the quilt. Make 25 sets of 4 matching red-and-cream hour glass units.

C Repeat with the green 3¼″ × 3¼″ squares to make 24 sets of 4 matching green-and-cream hour glass units.

D Layer a red 5¼″ × 5¼″ square right sides together with a cream 5¼″ × 5¼″ square. Cut on the diagonal twice with to yield 4 pairs of triangles. Sew the triangles together as before to make 2 matching hour glass units. The units will measure 4½″ × 4½″ and finish 4″ × 4″ in the quilt. Make 65. You'll use 25 hour glass units for the blocks and 40 for the pieced border. There will be 2 extra red and 2 extra cream triangles to use in another project.

E Repeat with the green 5¼″ × 5¼″ squares to make 60 green-and-cream hour glass units. You'll use 24 for the blocks and 36 for the pieced border.

Blocks

F Sew 4 matching red 1½″ × 4½″ rectangles and 4 matching green 1½″ × 4½″ rectangles together in pairs to make side units. Make a set of 4 side units for each block, or 49 sets total.

G H Lay out 4 matching red 2½″ hour glass units, 4 matching side units, and a red 4½″ hour glass unit. Sew together as shown in the diagram. The block will measure 8½″ × 8½″ and finish 8″ × 8″ in the quilt. Make 25 red blocks.

I Lay out 4 matching green 2½″ hour glass units, 4 matching side units, and a green 4½″ hour glass unit. Sew the units together as before. Make 24 green blocks.

Quilt Assembly

Lay out the blocks in 7 rows of 7 blocks each, alternating red and green. Add the cream tone-on-tone sashing rectangles and the red and green 2½″ × 2½″ cornerstones. Pay attention to color placement shown on the quilt assembly diagram. (You'll have extra red and green squares that will be used in the outer border.) Join into rows, pressing toward the sashing. Join the rows to complete the quilt center. Press.

Inner Borders

Join the red 1½″-wide inner border strips end to end with straight seams to make a border length approximately 300″ long. Press the seams open. Repeat with the green strips.

Lay the quilt center on the floor, smoothing it gently; do not tug or pull. Measure the quilt through the center from top to bottom *and* side to side. Both measurements should be 72½″, or close to that.

Sew the red strip and green strips together lengthwise and cut the pieced border into 4 strips each 72½″ long. Pin the borders to the sides, with right sides together and matching centers and ends. Make sure the green strip is next to the quilt center. Ease where necessary to fit. Press the seams toward the borders.

J Sew 2 red 1½″ × 1½″ squares and 2 green 1½″ × 1½″ squares together to make a Four-Patch block. Make 4. Sew a block to each end of the top and bottom borders, paying attention to color placement. Pin and sew the top and bottom borders so that the green is next to the quilt center, matching centers and ends and easing where necessary to fit. Press the seams toward the borders.

Outer Border

Refer to the quilt assembly diagram to join 10 red hour glass units and 9 green hour glass units to make a border. Make 4.

Pin and sew the borders to the quilt sides, matching centers and ends. Ease where necessary to fit. Press the seams toward the borders.

K Sew 2 red 2½″ × 2½″ squares and 2 green 2½″ × 2½″ squares together to make a Four-Patch block. Make 4. Sew a block to each end of the top and bottom borders, paying attention to color placement. Pin and sew the top and bottom borders to the quilt, matching centers and ends and easing where necessary to fit. Press the seams toward the borders.

Finishing

Layer, quilt, and bind as desired.

Jingle Bell Square was quilted in sand-colored thread in an edge-to-edge design called *Holly Berries* by Patricia E. Ritter of Urban Elementz.

A scrappy red binding is a great finish! Sew the red 2″ strips together diagonally end to end to make 1 long strip approximately 360″ long. I cut binding strips 2″ wide and sew the binding to the quilt with a ¼″ seam. This gives me a binding that finishes at ¼″ and doesn't nip off the corners of my patchwork units.

AT A GLANCE

A

Hour glass assembly

B

Small red hour glass unit

2½″ × 2½″ unfinished

Make 25 sets of 4 matching units.

C

Small green hour glass unit

2½″ × 2½″ unfinished

Make 24 sets of 4 matching units.

D

Large red hour glass unit

4½″ × 4½″ unfinished

Make 65.

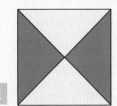

E

Large green hour glass unit

4½″ × 4½″ unfinished

Make 60.

F

Block side unit

2½″ × 4½″ unfinished

Make 49 sets of 4 matching units.

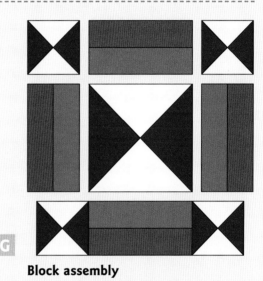

G

Block assembly

H

Red Jingle Bell Square block

8½″ × 8½″ unfinished

Make 25.

Green Jingle Bell Square block

8½″ × 8½″ unfinished

Make 24.

Small four-patch unit

2½″ × 2½″ unfinished

Make 4.

Large four-patch unit

4½″ × 4½″ unfinished

Make 4.

Quilt assembly

About Bonnie K. Hunter

Bonnie K. Hunter is passionate about quiltmaking, focusing mainly on scrap quilts with the simple feeling of "making do." She began her love affair with quilting in a home economics class during her senior year of high school in 1980 and has never looked back.

Dedicated to continuing the traditions of quilting, Bonnie enjoys meeting with quilters, teaching workshops, and lecturing to quilt guilds worldwide—challenging quilters to break the rules, think outside the box, and find what brings them joy.

Bonnie's favorite motto? "The Best Things in Life are Quilted!" of course!

Website: www.quiltville.com

Resources

Specialty Rulers

fast2cut Bonnie K. Hunter's Essential Triangle Tool
C&T Publishing   ctpub.com

Foundation Piecing Paper

Carol Doak's Foundation Paper
C&T Publishing   ctpub.com

Quilting Designs

Patricia E. Ritter   urbanelementz.com
patricia@urbanelementz.com

Hermione Agee   lorienquilting.com
hermione@lorienquilting.com

Jessica Schick   digitechpatterns.com
info@digitechpatterns.com

Susan Joy Noyes   ShowcaseQuilting.com
Contact_SDE@ShowcaseQuilting.com

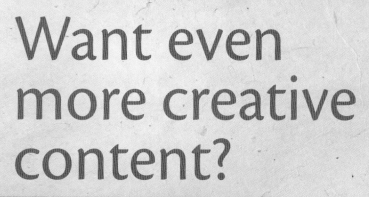

Want even more creative content?

Go to ctpub.com/offer

& sign up to receive our gift to you!

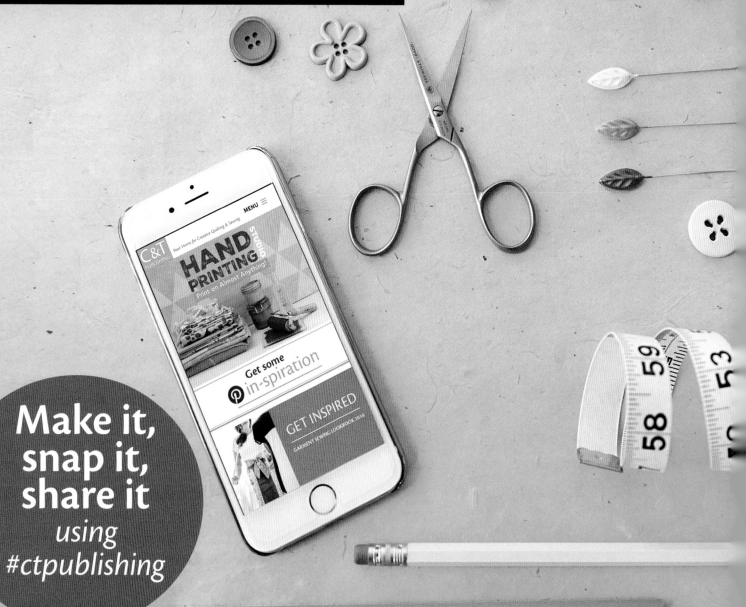

Make it, snap it, share it *using* #ctpublishing